GARLAND STUDIES ON THE ELDERLY IN AMERICA

edited by

STUART BRUCHEY
UNIVERSITY OF MAINE

A GARLAND SERIES

DOUBLE JEOPARDY

Resources and Minority Elders

MARY ANNE P. SALMON

GARLAND PUBLISHING, Inc.
New York & London / 1994

Library of Congress Cataloging-in-Publication Data

Salmon, Mary Anne P., 1948–
Double jeopardy : resources and minority elders / Mary Anne P. Salmon.
p. cm. — (Garland studies on the elderly in America)
Includes bibliographical references and index.
ISBN 0–8153–1712–3 (alk. paper)
1. Minority aged—United States—Economic conditions. 2. Retirement income—United States. 3. Old age assistance—United States. I. Title. II. Series.
HQ1064.U5S244 1994 94–12764
305.38'9664—dc20 CIP

Printed on acid-free, 250-year-life paper
Manufactured in the United States of America

To my mother and my other mother—

Mary Pierce Kniseley

and

Frances S. Cloe

Contents

Preface

Older African American and Hispanic adults have often been characterized as suffering from *double jeopardy*. Cross-sectional data have shown that they are poorer than either whites their own age or younger members of their own ethnic group. This book is a comparison of the double jeopardy and leveling hypotheses as they apply to the financial resources of older African Americans, Hispanics, and non-Hispanic whites. It uses Public Use Sample Census Data from 1960, 1970, 1980, and 1990 to provide a picture of three ten-year cohorts (born in the three decades between 1896 and 1925) and how their relative income has changed as they age.

This book was originally written as a dissertation in satisfaction of requirements for a Ph.D. in Sociology at the University of North Carolina, Chapel Hill, submitted in December 1985. The primary revisions made since then are the inclusion of the 1990 data for the same cohorts. In many cases, the additional observations enhanced patterns identified in the original work, and in others, the pattern became more ambiguous. These additional observations and their interpretation are integrated into Chapters 4 through 6. This preface is used to review some of the trends in the literature of the decade that has intervened since the original research.

Trends in the Literature of Ethnicity and Aging

Within any academic field, there are shifting trends in themes and foci. Gelfand and Barresi (1987) characterize three decades of interest in ethnogerontology. The 1960s, they say, were a time of great interest in ethnicity and race, concurrent with the civil rights movement. The 1970s were a time when interest peaked, except for a flurry of renewed interest in white ethnic groups. They say that in the 1980s there were two camps, those who, following Wilson's lead (1980), believed that variables related to social class had replaced ethnicity as a determinant of inequality and those who pointed out the continued discrimination in many areas of life.

According to Gelfand and Barresi's scheme, this book is squarely within the traditions of the decade in which the research originated. It weighs the relative contributions of ethnicity and a variety of other traditional correlates of social class to financial resources in later life. The conceptual framework for the analysis was provided by the competing ideas of double jeopardy and leveling—ideas that were in vogue among gerontologists at the time.

In early 1986, Coon published an article that proposed "to critically evaluate the merit of the concept of 'double jeopardy' as regards minority aged." His evaluation identified education, family, employment, income, and health-related issues as the areas of aging relevant to the topic, and after reviewing the inconsistent and often methodologically limited research in these areas, he went on to question the relevance and accuracy of the framework. He proposed that status inconsistency, exchange theory, and status generalization theory could profitably and more fruitfully be brought to the prediction and interpretation of differences among older adults of different ethnic groups.

Although the term *double jeopardy* appears in the literature up to the present, Coon appears to be the last person publishing in mainstream gerontological journals to address the accuracy or usefulness of the concept in a serious and systematic way as it applies to the area of income and resources. Belgrave and her colleagues explored similar ground among health-related variables in an attempt to explain ethnic differences in nursing home use, but they used a very broad definition of double jeopardy (1993).

The term has continued to be used descriptively for a variety of situations in which a group of people is disadvantaged by two ascribed statuses devalued by other segments of the society, in and out of the field of gerontology. For example, some form of double or multiple jeopardy has been used to characterize the systematic barriers raised against African American women of all ages (King, 1988); mental health service use among aging women (Rodeheaver and Datan, 1988); and the economic and service disadvantages of rural, minority elders (Bane, 1991). However, it is only within the area of health and health services that the term continues to be used fairly widely in the gerontological literature (Belgrave et al., 1993; Ferraro, 1987; Padgett, 1988).

This persistence into the 1990s of articles about double jeopardy in health status, or, more broadly, about ethnic differences in health status appears to be sparked in part by a methodological question. How should researchers interpret observed ethnic differences in self-reported health among ethnic groups in general and the cross-over effect of better health status among the oldest old members of minority groups? To what degree do they reflect subjective differences resulting from a lifetime of poorer economic well-being, health care, and living conditions; and to what extent do they reflect different cultural norms and expectations about either interpreting or reporting health status? (See Ford et al., 1990; Gibson, 1991a; Gibson and Burns, 1991; Johnson and Wolinsky, 1994.)

An interest in the interplay of ethnic and socioeconomic factors did not disappear with the diminished status of the term *double jeopardy*. As late as 1993, in a study of life satisfaction among white and African American elders, Krause wrote, "Instead of pitting race against these economic variables in their analyses, a more meaningful approach may involve tracing the effects of race on life satisfaction that operate indirectly through these economic factors." Some of the scholarship in this area continues to focus on issues of equality or equity (Dressel, 1988; Madison, 1992). Further, there are occasional articles that look at current trends and try to predict the future of ethnic inequalities (Dressel, 1986; Gibson and Burns, 1991; Torres-Gil, 1986; Watson, 1986). However, most mentions of ethnic economic differences appear as background information for policy or to explain ethnic differences in other life situations (Belgrave et al., 1993; Ford et al., 1990; Krause, 1993; Taeuber, 1990).

Some of this change in the focus of literature on ethnic differences may stem from the conception that differences are well understood and only need occasional updating. However, some portion of the shift in focus must be attributable to a conscious shift in the ethnic research agenda. Using the broad brush strokes of Gelfand and Barresi, we might characterize the 1990s as the decade of cultural diversity.

In a book review essay in 1989, Green closes the door to the focus on social justice and opens the door to diversity, writing, "The authors [of four books under review] further note that most of this [past] literature concerns the special disabilities that accompany aging for minority persons, an extension in one form or another of the well-known multiple jeopardy hypothesis." He goes on to explain that this approach leads to the view of ethnicity as a social problem.

In a similar vein, Stanford and Yee, in an issue of *Generations* devoted to cultural diversity, wrote, "Unfortunately, many smaller populations have been defined by comparison with the majority population (e.g., African Americans were compared to whites with regard to socioeconomic status, use of services, service need, and patterns of informal caregiving and support)" (1991, p. 12).

Some of the literature of the 1990s that appears under the heading of cultural diversity seems to be the old wine of ethnic comparisons in new wine skins of diversity. However, there *has* been a real increase in articles devoted to research within an ethnic population, not based on explicit or implicit comparison to whites. Examples of this include perceptions of retirement among African Americans (Gibson, 1991b), migration patterns of older Hispanics and African Americans (Biafora and Longino, 1990; Longino and Smith, 1991), and religiosity among African Americans (Levin and Taylor, 1993).

Ethnogerontology is broadened and enriched by the focus on diversity. It highlights the variety *within* individual cultures. It explores the beliefs and coping mechanisms of smaller ethnic groups such as Laotians, Guatemalans, and Cambodians. Most importantly, it facilitates research into the contributions and strengths of African American and Hispanic elders, not merely their disadvantages and social problems. Still, a disdain for the questions of inequities would be premature. Interethnic comparisons of income, health, service access, or any other societal goods will only become irrelevant when ethnic differences no longer exist. Until then, aging policy must recognize and address these inequities.

Recent Changes in the World of Minority Elders

Increased Affluence

Since the early 1980s, the trend of more affluent cohorts reaching retirement ages has continued for older adults as a whole (Hurd, 1989). As a result, the poverty rate for people over 65 is the same as or lower than for people under 65 (Cutler, 1991; U.S. Senate Special Committee on Aging et al., 1991, p. 41). This, in turn, has continued to inspire questions about intergenerational equity (Cutler, 1991; Kamikawa, 1991; Minkler, 1991) and questions of entitlement (Cutler, 1991).

As Cutler argues, however, the successful reduction of poverty among older adults has been very uneven. African American, Hispanic, and other ethnic minority elders continue to have very high poverty rates. Minkler (1991) goes on to argue that the whole question of intergenerational equity is based on a "flawed and dangerous" premise. She suggests that poverty among the young is due to economic market factors such as inflation, plant closings, the rise in jobs that pay less than minimum wage, a decline in the real income of young men, and the increase in female-headed households. These are factors completely unrelated to entitlements for older adults.

Increase in the Hispanic Population

The last decade has seen both growth and dispersion of the Hispanic population in the United States (Kanellos, 1993, p. 335). Although their numbers remain relatively small, older Hispanics are the fastest growing group of elders. In addition, increased immigration from Central American countries makes for greater diversity *within* the group, hitherto composed largely of people of Mexican, Puerto Rican, and Cuban descent (Biafora and Longino, 1990; Minkler, 1991; U.S. Senate Special Committee on Aging et al., 1991, p. 14).

Changes in the African American Grandmother Pattern

The pattern of African American women assuming primary child-rearing responsibilities for their grandchildren is old and well-documented. However, the past decade has seen a sad alteration in that pattern, occasioned by the epidemic of crack cocaine addiction in some parts of the African American community and to a lesser extent by the spread of AIDS among intravenous drug users. (This is not to imply that either issue is limited to the African American community, but that the involvement of grandmothers in raising the children of the victims has only been documented for this community.)

Under the traditional pattern, the children's mothers have remained involved in child rearing. The grandparents have either had exclusive responsibility for a limited period of time (e.g., while the parents moved north in search of work) or had shared responsibility with the children's mother (e.g., while a young mother remained at home and completed her education). These patterns still occur, but in the case of drug addiction, the grandmother is often receiving no help from the mother, who is dysfunctional if she remains alive (Burton, 1992; Minkler et al., 1992).

The Persistence of Ethnic Inequity

As this book illustrates, the essential ethnic inequities that inspired the original dissertation continue into the 1990s. African American elders continue to have lower incomes, higher poverty rates, greater dependence in their living arrangements, and fewer resources than their white counterparts. While aging appears to have a leveling effect at the end of a lifetime of inequity, the effect of race persists when other socioeconomic variables are controlled. Further, the educational and income patterns of younger cohorts do not suggest substantially greater equality in the future. The picture for Hispanics is more mixed, and it is complicated by changes in the public sample, and the heterogeneity of the population. Nonetheless, it still suggests a need to be concerned with inequities in the resources of Hispanic elders as this group continues to grow.

In reaching for the more complete picture given us by the literature of cultural diversity in the 1990s, let us not completely turn our backs on the civil rights–inspired documentation of social injustice that rose from the 1960s. The issues raised then have not become less important for becoming less fashionable.

Acknowledgments

A proper thank you to all of the people who helped make this book possible, from the original dissertation research to its current incarnation, would probably be as long as the book. I continue to get by with a *lot* of help from my friends.

Thanks first to my dissertation committee chair, Peter Uhlenberg, for his creative ideas, his excellent academic guidance, his acute editorial comments, and his unflagging moral support. I could not have chosen a better person or scholar as a role model. I was also extremely fortunate in my committee, at the University of North Carolina Department of Sociology, Richard Cramer, François Nielsen, Rachel Rosenfeld, and Harvey Smith.

Thanks for material, intellectual, and social support to the leadership and staff of the Center for Aging Research and Educational Services (CARES) at the UNC School of Social Work, and of the Cecil G. Sheps Center for Health Services Research. Gary Nelson and Dennis Streets at CARES have allowed me time and facilities for the creation of the book, as Gordon DeFriese, Ned Brooks, and Vic Schoenbach of the Sheps Center did for the earlier work on the dissertation. Thanks to Carol Porter of the Sheps Center for teaching me the ways of macro-and microcomputers; and to Lynn Whitener, super librarian, for finding the unfindable at both points in time.

Special thanks are due to Frances Cloe and Carl D. Silver for financing the dissertation research, without which there could have been no book.

Ed Bachman, at the Institute for Research in the Social Sciences, arranged access to the 1990 Public Use Sample, and the Help Desk staff at the Office of Information Technology showed me how to download and transform the resulting data set for PC use.

Beautiful, brilliant, and sophisticated School of Social Work graduate students, Christina Jacobs and Marni Thompson, provided invaluable library research.

Thanks to Karen Troy for chauffeur service, word processing, and general hand-holding at the dissertation stage, and wry encouragement with the book (mostly by not letting me come out and play until it was finished). For additional hand-holding, shoulder-crying, and words of sanity at one time or the other, thanks to Judith, Ursula, Elizabeth, Carla, and HP.

Margaret Morse bravely combined the roles of copyeditor and friend—giving up evenings and weekends to find my mistakes, and often suffering the fate of other bearers of bad news. The correctly spelled, hyphenated, and punctuated words are hers. The errors are there because I second-guessed her recommendations.

In the first-shall-be-last department, I would like to thank my family. My family of origin all gave me love and support, but my mother and sisters (Mary Kniseley, Kathy Douberly, and Annette Lancaster) also helped type and proof the original dissertation.

Thanks to my daughter, Ethel Myers, who grew into womanhood in the shadow of this research, for material help at the dissertation stage and telephone reassurance through the preparation of the book. (Sometimes we older parents need that service.)

Thanks to my husband, Kevin, for many hours of toil at the word processor at the dissertation stage (completely above and beyond the call of duty), for hours of additional proofreading at the book stage, for being an endless font of arcane and esoteric information; and for sustaining me in mind, body, and spirit. In other words, thanks to Kevin, without whom . . .

Figures and Tables

Double Jeopardy

I
The Theory and Context of Double Jeopardy

Growing old is often accompanied by a deterioration of the resources that were built up earlier in life. A large amount of power and wealth is controlled by a few older people in the United States; but for every septuagenarian who wields power and amasses fortunes in government and board room, there are thousands who must economize to live on pensions without selling their houses and many more for whom such a pension and home ownership represent enviable wealth. Old age is a time of decreasing opportunity to pursue new sources of revenue and increasing catastrophic threats to the resources already acquired. What, then, does growing older mean for ethnic and racial minority groups who have faced special barriers to obtaining resources throughout their lives?

The financial plight of minority elders has been characterized as *double jeopardy*, but that term, as ordinarily used, has more attention-getting than explanatory value. If, as it is sometimes used, double jeopardy merely means that older African Americans, Hispanics, and other people of color are more financially disadvantaged than both their younger counterparts and their white age mates, then it is undoubtedly true (Dowd and Bengtson, 1978; Jackson, 1972 and 1980; Kent, 1971a; Moore, 1971; National Council on Aging, 1972; Palmore and Manton, 1973; Pampel, 1981). But there are more interesting and puzzling questions about the equity or inequity of income distribution among older adults from ethnic minorities.

This book uses Public Use Sample data from the U.S. decennial census to examine the distribution of income among African Americans, Hispanics, and whites as they age. Four central sets of questions frame this work:

1. What are the income differences among ethnic groups in the preretirement ages? What are the sociodemographic variables that help to explain these differences in income?

2. How do the income differences among ethnic groups change as cohorts age? Is any formulation of the "double jeopardy" hypothesis supported by these changes? Do variables that help explain ethnic differences among preretirement age groups gain, lose, or maintain their explanatory power as the cohorts age?

3. What other types of financial resources reduce or increase inequality among ethnic groups? Other assets? Political policies and government programs? Family assistance and living arrangements?

4. What do the findings of this research, in light of the current trends among younger African Americans and Hispanics, suggest about the future of minority elders in the United States?

This chapter presents a theoretical framework for the book. It begins with a discussion of the roles of age and ethnicity in the distributive system, drawing heavily on the work of Lenski (1966) and Wilson (1978). The focus then narrows to the double jeopardy hypothesis with a description of its several formulations and a review of the literature. After describing the universe of the study, including the historical background of the study cohorts, it concludes with a preview of the remaining chapters.

Aging, Ethnicity, and the Distributive System

To understand the distribution of resources to minority elders, it is necessary to look at the special place of ethnicity and age within the distributive system. Lenski has argued that (1) in any society, the distributive system contains a number of separate class hierarchies based on different sources of power; (2) each person in the society holds simultaneous positions in each hierarchy; (3) boundaries within systems vary in permeability so that castelike positions may coexist with strata from which mobility is possible; and (4) conflict and competition for society's goods exist not only among strata within a given hierarchy, but also among hierarchical systems. The degree to which position in one hierarchy determines positions in the others varies both among societies and among hierarchies. For the United States, Lenski identifies at least six such power/class systems: occupational, property, educational attainment, gender, racial/ethnic, and age (Lenski, 1966, pp. 79–82). Two more systems might be added to these—political/legal and family/social. Bengtson (1979, p. 16) recognizes this multidimensional system as the one appropriate for the study of ethnic aging, although he does not directly credit Lenski.

Matilda White Riley and other proponents of age-stratification theory emphasize status or power rather than the distribution of material goods. They argue that the United States is an age-graded society with age segregation in every facet of life and that age assumes particular importance around such life cycle transitions as graduation, entering the labor force, or retirement (Riley, 1971a?). There is no clear attempt in Riley's work to integrate age and class systems despite her use of the term age-stratification. However, in his review of the age-stratification literature Dowd (1980) suggests that income is the primary source of power between graduation and retirement. Before graduation and after retirement, age status (childhood or old age) represents powerlessness to a degree that overshadows most other measures of power.[1]

While there is intuitive appeal in Dowd's suggestion, it oversimplifies the determinants of power. Lenski's scheme, on the other hand, allows for the complexities of real life. Here the relevance of age, like that of the other hierarchies, may change over the life course of people and over historical time.

Lenski tells us that over historical time there are continuous struggles to alter the salience of particular power class systems. The liberal movement of the last two centuries has essentially been an attempt to discredit those hierarchies which are most clearly based on ascription and support those based, at least in principle, upon achievement. As a result, in the United States, within the lifetime of today's older adults, there has been some discrediting of sex and ethnicity as legitimate power bases. As these sources of power are declared suspect, education and occupation become more important.

This societal shift toward achievement orientation does not eliminate, or even necessarily reduce, the financial disadvantages of minority groups. Historical patterns of discrimination have created the conditions for a castelike underclass such as Wilson describes (1978). Indeed, Wilson's argument is quite consistent with Lenski's model. He demonstrates that as race becomes less important in the distribution of income, those people who have been denied education and desirable occupations because of the salience of race in the past are now denied a larger share of material goods on the basis of their low educational and occupational strata rather than their racial status. He does not use Lenski's terms as I have done here, but translating his major premise into these terms does it no violence whatever.

Within a given person's lifetime, historical changes such as those described above occur. In addition, there are two ways in which the significance of a particular hierarchy may change for that individual in the course of his or her lifetime:

(1) *Position in the age hierarchy influences the possibility of mobility in certain of the other hierarchies.* For example, one's place in the educational hierarchy may continue to be important throughout life, but mobility in this hierarchy is available and "appropriate" primarily for the young. Those who pursue education later in life may forego a certain amount of age status and may receive less chance of occupational mobility from these gains in education than would a younger person attaining the same educational status.

(2) *Position in the age hierarchy determines which power hierarchies have important consequences for the individual.* In other words, power/class structures have different weights for different age strata. For example, employment/occupation may become more important than property and wealth as a societal basis for the distribution of goods. However, if that society has mandatory retirement, both the status and the financial benefits of occupation dwindle when the retirement age is reached, and one might expect that wealth and property will be more important in determining the financial well-being of older adults than that of society as a whole.

This conception of the stratification system provides a background for the specific questions of interest in this book. While it is not possible to test directly the operation of competing hierarchies, variables representing the hierarchies of occupation, education, age, sex, region, and race can be used to trace the interplay between these hierarchies in the life course of today's older adults. This knowledge, in turn, gives insights about the mechanisms through which these hierarchies interact to determine the place of individuals in the distributive system—specifically, individuals who suffer the combined disadvantages of racial/ethnic minority status and postretirement age.

The Double Jeopardy Hypothesis

Definition

The literature about the ethnic elderly that has dealt with stratification has been aimed at determining the relative equity of distribution. There is general agreement that: (1) African Americans and Hispanics fare worse than non-Hispanic whites in the society as a whole; (2) older adults fare worse than younger adults; and (3) minority elders fare worse than elders in the dominant group (Dowd and Bengtson, 1978; Jackson, 1972 and 1980; Kent, 1971a; Moore, 1971; National Council on Aging, 1972; Palmore and Manton, 1973; Pampel, 1981). However, there are two competing ideas (not quite hypotheses) about the relationship between age and ethnic status as they affect the distributive system.

Double jeopardy (also called multiple jeopardy or multiple hazards) is the view that those who have a disadvantaged ascribed status throughout life (race or gender for example) face greater losses in later years than their age-mates in the dominant group (Dowd and Bengtson, 1978; Jackson, 1980; National Council on Aging, 1972; Pampel, 1981). Since its introduction by the National Urban League in 1964, this term has appeared in much of the writing about ethnic elders, but it is seldom used with any degree of precision and is tested even less often. Jackson, for example, writes, ". . . the argument here is that older persons do not experience problems solely on the basis of age but that problems associated with age become increasingly difficult to resolve when they are compounded by institutionalized victimization" (1980, p. 56). It is unclear how this description of double jeopardy could be operationalized, but for Jackson it is a core assumption, not a proposition to be tested. Her monograph and articles go on to demonstrate clearly the disadvantaged status of aging African Americans, Asians, Native Americans, and Hispanics, as well as of non-Hispanic white women. They do not test whether these disadvantages are greater or smaller than those of younger minority group members relative to their white male counterparts.

It is not explicit in most descriptive works whether double jeopardy means that the effects of ethnicity and aging are simply additive or if they are interactive. In two cases in which the idea is empirically tested, the authors disagree about the definition. Contrasting definitions are best shown by the three graphs in Figures 1-1 through 1-3.[2]

Figure 1-1. Model of Double Jeopardy

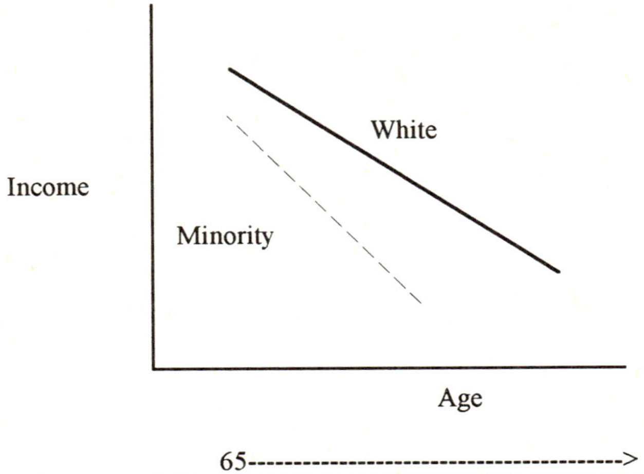

Figure 1-1 shows a negative interaction between age and minority status. After age 65, aging causes income to decline for both groups, but the decline is more severe for the minority group as indicated by the steeper slope of the minority income line. All would agree that this case constitutes double jeopardy.

There is disagreement, however, regarding how the case represented by figure 1-2 should be labeled. Here the effects of age and minority status are completely independent. Though both groups experience income decline with age, the income of one group relative to the other remains unchanged. Dowd and Bengtson (1978) include this case in their definition of double jeopardy, but Pampel (1981) explicitly rejects it. I have labeled this case *parallel jeopardy* to distinguish it from the situation pictured in figure 1-1.

Figure 1-2. Model of Parallel Jeopardy

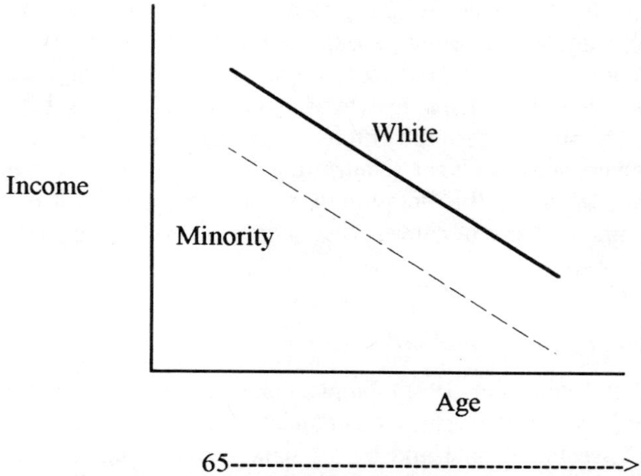

Figure 1-3. Model of Leveling

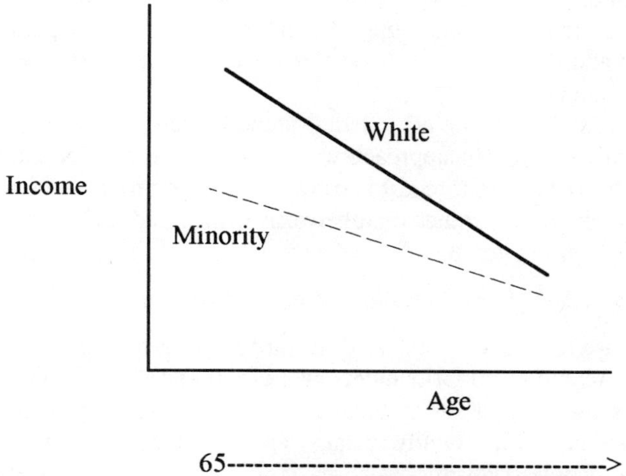

Figure 1-3 represents the antithesis of double jeopardy, the idea of *leveling*. In leveling there is a negative interaction between age and *majority* status. As in the other two hypothetical cases, both groups experience income decline after age 65. However, here the decline is more severe for the majority group, which leads to greater income equality with age among ethnic groups in the same cohorts. If this is true, older minority group members might still have fewer material goods than older non-Hispanic whites, but the differences between them would be smaller than the differences between those same groups when members were younger (controlling for inflation). Leveling is more clearly defined in the literature than multiple jeopardy. It is clear that only some measure of convergence, not cross-over, is required for leveling to exist.

The Empirical Findings on Double Jeopardy

Dowd and Bengtson (1978) found support for their formulation of double jeopardy, but their study was handicapped by the inappropriate use of cross-sectional data and by a small, geographically localized sample. Palmore and Manton's work using their "Equality Index" (1973) does not directly test double jeopardy in any of the formulations described above. However, comparing the resources of older African American women with those of young white men, and finding virtually no area of overlap, they conclude that there are additive effects of race and age (and sex) that support a multiple jeopardy hypothesis. Like Dowd and Bengtson, they have used cross-sectional data to examine a longitudinal question.

Pampel (1981), on the other hand, found evidence of leveling using longitudinal data. His approach was sound, but because of sample-size limitations he was forced to make a crude comparison between whites and nonwhites, rather than between whites and any other specific racial or ethnic group.

Factors That Might Work to Produce Double Jeopardy

There are four factors that work toward making old age a greater financial hardship to minority elders as a group and therefore provide support for an expectation of double jeopardy. These represent the hierarchies of sex, family/social, and wealth, as well as occupation/income. They are:

1. *Lower sex ratio*: The lowering of the sex ratio in postretirement years has negative social and financial conse-

quences for the older population. African Americans have a lower sex ratio (smaller number of men per 100 women) than either Hispanics or non-Hispanic whites (U.S. Bureau of the Census, 1984). Since women in the U.S. fare worse economically than men, this might be expected to decrease average income after 65 for African Americans. On the other hand, Hispanics have a larger number of men per 100 women than whites.

2. *The "African American grandmother pattern":* In 1974, 26 percent of African Americans over 65 were raising grandchildren in their home, compared to only 15 percent of whites (Jackson and Wood, 1976). This constitutes a financial drain on the resources of older blacks. (This difference should appear in poverty data but not in income data.)

3. *Different levels of investments/accumulation of wealth*: Whites accumulate more wealth and property over a lifetime of earnings than minority groups. These may become income resources, or in smaller amounts, emergency funds for retired whites.

4. *Pensions*: Because of their employment in the lowest sector of a fragmented labor market during most of their labor force years, minority elders are less likely to qualify for private pensions and receive lower average benefits when they do qualify.

Factors That Might Work to Produce Leveling

Pampel summarizes the usual argument for leveling: "Since there is less income to be unequally distributed among old people than among young people, age [*sic*; this is clearly intended to read *race*] and sex inequalities will be reduced during old age" (1981 p.142). This suggestion of a ceiling or regression effect is unsatisfactory because it implies that a fixed sum exists as the total income available to older adults at any one time. The further implication of such an idea is that the financial gain of one older person or group creates financial loss for another.

In reality, a fixed sum only exists when an economy is not expanding, and when it does exist, it remains to be divided among society as a whole. Older people can make gains at the expense of other groups rather than at each other's. However, retirement from paid employment works to reduce the variance in the resources of older adults, which creates the appearance of an income ceiling. Interest, savings, rents, dividends, royalties, and similar income from wealth are available to those of any age, and indeed the fourth factor mentioned above argues that ethnic differences in the possession of these may contribute to double jeopardy.

If, on the other hand, a preponderance of the people in this country are entirely dependent on the direct returns of their occupations, then *leveling should be expected.* This is because the difference between a very good pension and the minimum Social Security payment, or even Supplementary Security Income, is much smaller than the difference between a very good salary and the minimum wage. Large amounts of wealth in this country are in the hands of older adults, but this is limited to such a small proportion of the population that when people rather than dollars are the unit of analysis, wealth may prove to have relatively little impact on the overall well-being of any ethnic group.

While the movement from salary to some combination of pension and accumulated wealth as the primary source of financial resources is the strongest argument for leveling, there are two other potential sources for this pattern:

1. *Narrowing of the ethnic differences in marital disruption*: At every age from 25 on, whites are more likely than Hispanics, and Hispanics more likely than African Americans, to be married with a spouse present. However, the magnitude of ethnic differences begins decreasing in late middle age and continues to do so after age 65 (U.S. Bureau of the Census, 1984, table 264). Therefore, the groups should draw closer in their experience of marital disruption over time.

2. *Government transfer payments:* If government transfers to older adults reach those in greatest need, this should also contribute to leveling because minority resources are smaller both before and after retirement ages.

The Jeopardy of Poverty

The double jeopardy hypothesis focuses on relative levels of income and does not deal with the question of income adequacy. A very small proportionate or even absolute difference may mean the difference between living in modest comfort and wanting for necessities. Although it is only a statistical approximation of this qualitative difference, the federal poverty line provides a measure of income adequacy that has the added advantage of being adjusted for family size.

Given this, a second hypothesis of jeopardy versus leveling can be tested—the jeopardy of poverty. As ethnic populations age, do differences in poverty rates increase, remain the same, or decrease?

Historical Context: The Study Population

Because of the interplay among aging, history, and cohort effects, it is impossible to talk generally about the life experience of young people without specifying when they were young and when old. Therefore, although the nature of the sample will be discussed at length in Chapter 2, it is necessary to precede a discussion of the research questions, to be addressed in Chapters 3 through 6 with a description of the people about whom these questions are being asked.

Table 1-1. Historical Events in the Lives of the Study Population

		Ages of Cohorts		
Event	*Year*	*A*	*B*	*C*
U.S. enters World War I	1917	12–21	2–11	0–1
Mandatory school attendance laws in all states	1918	13–22	3–12	0–2
Great flu epidemic	1919	14–23	4–13	0–3
Women vote	1920	15–24	5–14	0–4
U.S./Mexican border patrol established	1924	19–28	9–18	0–8
Stock market crash	1929	24–33	14–23	4–13
CIO organized	1938	33–42	23–32	13–22
U.S. enters World War II	1941	36–45	26–35	16–25
Brown v. Board of Education	1954	49–58	39–48	29–38
Civil Rights Act of 1964 (public accommodations)	1964	59–68	49–58	39–48
Voting Rights Act	1965	60–69	50–59	40–49

The population of interest is Hispanic, African American, and non-Hispanic white men and women who were ages 55 to 84 in 1980; that is, those who were born between 1896 and 1925. They are divided into three birth cohorts: Cohort A, born 1896 to 1905; Cohort B, born 1906 to 1915; and Cohort C, born 1916 to 1925. Table 1-1 presents the ages of these cohorts during some key historical events, to help provide some historical perspective on the times which shaped their lives. Expectations and findings in each of the research questions inevitably will be influenced by historical context.

Distributive Hierarchies: The Years before Retirement

A thorough study of the determinants of ethnic income differences for the general population is a mammoth project, far beyond the scope of this book. Still, a brief examination of these differences within the cohorts represented here is necessary to establish a baseline against which the effects of aging can be studied. What, then, are these differences among ethnic groups along the dimensions of stratification we have theorized—racial/ethnic, property, education, occupation, and gender?[3] It can be argued that the ethnic hierarchy was quite strong during the period when these three cohorts grew up, were educated, and began their careers, but the direct and indirect influences of race/ethnicity are hard to separate.

Property. Indirect influences are those which operated through the other hierarchical systems. For example, property in the form of hereditary wealth was not forbidden to African Americans, but neither was it widespread among members of these cohorts only a few generations removed from slavery.

Hispanics with hereditary wealth were, in most cases, less likely than those who were poor to migrate to the United States. However, many older Hispanics in these cohorts were not migrants or even descendants of migrants in our current understanding of those terms. Parts of California and all of Arizona and New Mexico became United States territory only 47 years before the oldest members of Cohort A were born.[4] Furthermore, the U.S./Mexican border did not exist in its modern form until the border patrol was established in 1924, when members of Cohort A (the oldest cohort) were 19 to 28 years old. Until that time movement of families and individuals across the border was frequent and casual (Samora, 1975). Descendants of Hispanic residents of these territories represented the upper and lower strata of a nearly feudal distributive system (Samora, 1975).

A second exception to the general poverty of Hispanics in the United States came with the influx of wealthy and upper-middle-class

Cubans after Fidel Castro came to power in 1959, but Cubans have never constituted a large segment of the Hispanic population in the United States.

Education. Education was much more an indication of one's family's rank in the hierarchy of property than an independent route to advancement in the stratification system when the oldest of the three cohorts attended school. Although public high school was the accepted form of secondary education in New England by the time of the Civil War, many of the member of Cohorts A and B did not have an opportunity to attend. In the 1917–1918 school year, 9.3 percent of the U.S. school population was enrolled in high school, but only 5.1 percent of the school population in the South. As an educator wrote in 1922, ". . . in many counties throughout the South not a single standard public four-year high school has yet been established" (Knight, 1922).

College was still largely the domain of the wealthy. For those who were not college-bound, the merits of high school were ambiguous, as the debate between "preparation for college and preparation for life" raged on as a major educational controversy (Johnson et al., 1969). Large families (as well as the Great Depression for the middle and part of the youngest cohort) furnished economic incentives for young people to begin their working lives young (Kett, 1977). For older generations raised on Horatio Alger,[5] hard work, rather than education, was the perceived path to upward mobility. By the time the youngest of the three cohorts was educated, public high school was widespread, and boys who discontinued their education to fight in World War II came back with G.I. college benefits. Norms of educational attainment changed (Johanningmeir, 1980). Younger cohorts would, increasingly, need formal education as certification of qualification for desirable jobs.

Although the Harlem Renaissance showed the world the potential for intellectual contributions from the African American community, education for this group was generally poorer in both quantity and quality than it was for whites in the same cohorts. Schools were "separate but equal" in the South, and nearly as segregated in the North where ethnic neighborhoods were served by ethnic schools (Wilson, 1978). The youngest person in these cohorts was 29 years old when *Brown v. Board of Education* started the long, slow process of achieving school integration. Financial pressure for young people to begin work early was at least as strong for African Americans as for whites, and except for a handful of businessmen and professionals who would form a small African American elite in major urban centers, the financial rewards of education for African Americans appeared dubious to many.

For Hispanics in these cohorts, perhaps to an even greater degree than for African Americans and whites, education reflects their parents' place in the stratification system. Because the middle class has historically been smaller in Latin America than in the United States, education and other measures of socioeconomic status among Hispanics in the United States may be distributed in such a way that a relatively small group scores quite high while a large groups scores very low. Old Spanish families in the United States, and prosperous immigrants from Latin countries should compare favorably with whites. Children of less fortunate Hispanic parents, especially those who represent the first and second generation in the United States, may have little or no education. The historical failure of public schools in the United States to provide adequate education for those with Spanish as a first language and a basic distrust of schools by Hispanic parents are two major reasons (Nava, 1975; Selakovich, 1978).

Occupation. Occupation was to become more dependent on education over the work history of these cohorts, and ethnic differences in that variable would take their toll, but the influence of race/ethnicity on occupation in these cohorts came in more direct fashion as well. Jim Crow laws were firmly in place in the South. Some of the people in Cohort A were in the first wave of African American migration northward to fill the labor gaps left by the restrictive immigration laws that followed World War I, but both native-born and immigrant whites resisted the hiring African Americans except for service jobs (Wilson, 1978). Employers did not hire African Americans and whites for the same job, either for fear of arousing workers' protest or for the advantages of threatening recalcitrant white workers with the hiring of African American replacements (Wilson, 1978).

When unskilled white workers were organized into the CIO in 1938, an important issue for which they bargained was the elimination of African American "scab" labor (Wilson, 1978). Only with the passing of the Wagner Act in 1935 did African American labor begin to have a voice. Although labor unions with African American membership experienced their strongest growth during the youth of these cohorts, many accepted the racial employment patterns in place. In 1944, when all of the three study cohorts were adult, this laissez-faire racial policy was cited in unions in the tobacco, textile, clothing, laundry, longshore, and bituminous coal industries (Northrup, 1944). Despite historical ethnic differences, past and present union membership for African Americans and whites in these cohorts is not very different. Only 18 percent of African Americans and 25 percent of whites age 65 and older in 1974 reported past or present union membership for anyone in their household (Jackson and Wood, 1976). After World War II, African Americans made additional modest gains in opportunity. Thus, the youngest cohort of African Americans (those in Cohort C) had relatively greater occupational advantages than their counterparts in the two older cohorts but still relatively few advantages relative to whites.

Hispanics, like African Americans, experienced direct discrimination in hiring; if they were immigrants, they faced the additional problems of language. However, like other immigrants, and unlike African Americans, those willing to improve their English and forego the outward signs of their cultural heritage could be assimilated into the mainstream.[6] Nevertheless, Hispanics, like African Americans in these cohorts, were most likely to be in service and unskilled industrial jobs. The use of seasonal farm workers, legal (braceros) and illegal, was also widespread, particularly in the West (Samora, 1975).

Special problems faced by minority groups in the occupational hierarchy include not only difficulty in getting hired for any job and being hired only for certain undesirable jobs, but also being the most likely to be laid off when economic times are bad. This may be the direct result of discrimination, but it is more often the result of the greater seniority of white workers. This, in turn, was caused by past discrimination in hiring (Wilson, 1978).

Gender. Gender, like race, is an ascriptive hierarchy that affects the workings of the other hierarchies. For women much more than for men, status and resources are determined by marital status as much as occupation and by the marital partner's occupation as much or more than own occupation. Women gained the vote when the oldest members of the oldest cohort were 24, and the youngest members of the youngest cohort were not yet born, but with that achievement, feminism was to become dormant for about forty years. Women worked outside the home throughout this period, and probably throughout history, but it was during the Great Depression that ". . . employment became more compelling to women and acceptable to their husbands, despite hostile sentiment in the community" (Elder, 1974). During and after World War II, married women begin working outside the home in large numbers even when their husbands made adequate wages (Kreps, 1976).

Women, like African Americans, were (and continued to be) hired for certain types of jobs reserved for them, although a wider variety of jobs (specifically, clerical jobs) became defined as women's jobs during the working life of these cohorts. By 1940, 45 percent of working women were in nonmanual jobs, most of them clerical (Kreps, 1976). Because the greatest number of women added to the labor force were married women with working husbands, the major effect was to increase the family income of those who were already receiving incomes that were at least adequate. For those women who never married or who were part of the increasing number of divorced people in these cohorts, occupation and income generally remained low regardless of education.

Marital disruption, then, is one aspect of the family/social hierarchy that particularly affects women. African American women in these cohorts are more likely to have experienced marital disruption than whites because of both high rates of widowhood (U.S. Bureau of the Census, 1984), and higher rates of separation and divorce for African Americans (Cherlin, 1981). Hispanic women in the United States have lower divorce rates than whites (possibly, in part, because of the influence of the Catholic Church), but they are less likely than whites to be married and living with a spouse at all but the youngest ages in these three cohorts.

Place of Residence. Besides the personal characteristics that influence one's place in the stratification system, there is regional and size-of-place stratification in this country. During the lifetime of these cohorts, the South has trailed the rest of the country in major measures of well-being including education, per capita income, and poverty rate (U.S. Bureau of the Census, 1984). Since African Americans are disproportionately located in the South, and two of the four states with the largest concentrations of Hispanics are also in the South,[7] place of residence adds to the list of disadvantages of these groups relative to the overall white population. The size-of-place effect has not been stable throughout the lifetime of these cohorts. Rural areas have always had economic disadvantages; but the "land of opportunity" has moved from the city to the non–central-city portion of metropolitan areas (National Committee against Discrimination in Housing, 1968). African Americans and Hispanics have been overrepresented in both the rural areas and the central cities, adding another layer of disadvantage.

Distributive Hierarchies: The Years after Retirement

Wealth. Assets, such as net worth and transfer payments, become relatively more important reflections of social status with aging, as retirement reduces current earned income (Moon, 1977; O'Rand, 1982; Projector and Weiss, 1966) Among those who have assets such as savings accounts, stock, and U.S. savings bonds, those who are 55 to 64 and 65 and over have higher mean and median dollar-value holdings than those 54 and younger. In 1977 the median savings account for those with such accounts was $6,250 for both those 55 to 64 and 65 and over while the median was only $1,500 for those younger than 55. Similarly, in the same year the median dollar value of stock held by 55 to 64 year-old stock holders was $12,800; for holders 65 and older, it was $13,000; and for holders younger than 55, it was only $3,000 (Duffy et al., 1980). These are the kinds of figures frequently cited in both popular and academic works to argue against what is seen as a misplaced societal concern for the financial well-being of older adults. (See, for example, AARP, 1985; Anderson, 1985; Duffey et al, 1980.) There are at least two problems with drawing such conclusions from these particular figures: (1) because only those who hold assets are being considered, there is no way of knowing the relative likelihood of holding such assets among the age groups; and (2) because everyone under age 54 is taken together, the lower median for younger people includes every child's "very own" savings account with $15 in it and the holdings of every person who receives one share of stock at birth, for graduation, or at some other point of passage.

Beyond considerations of the relative assets of younger people and older people, it is clear from these figures that the average person past retirement age who is fortunate enough to have savings and investments does not have enough to live on the interest or dividends or even regularly to supplement pension and social security income. At best, he or she has a small fund with which to meet emergencies.

A larger proportion of whites than African Americans have investments and savings. About 39 percent of whites over 65 in 1974 reported having savings, and 10 percent reported investments. For African Americans over 65 in the same survey, 8 percent reported savings, and 2 percent reported investments (Jackson and Wood, 1976). Data for Hispanics are not available from that survey, but intermediate levels consistent with other socioeconomic variables would be expected. Even if the holding of savings and investments were more evenly distributed, it is doubtful that the value of these assets for most of the older population would make significant differences in financial well-being.

Home ownership. The one asset that is both more widespread among older adults and of higher value among them is home equity. Seventy-three per cent of people over 65 own their homes, over 90 per cent of the total value of these homes is in the home owners' equity (Pies, 1984). In general, home equity has not been a very liquid asset, and its advantage, beyond assuring familiar surroundings, has been the elimination of rent from the older person's monthly living expenses. More recently, a number of plans are being implemented by government and commercial agencies to convert home equity into resources for the older person's lifetime—especially for the financing of long-term care for impaired elders. This adds an additional disadvantage to the older adult who does not own his or her home.

A rather large number of older southern, rural African Americans own their homes—often a home place for several generations, and sometimes substandard. Still, African Americans and Hispanics in these cohorts (and later cohorts as well) have faced overt discrimination in being allowed to purchase housing, above and beyond the barrier to home ownership inherent in poorer-paying jobs and more frequent layoffs. In 1974, 78 percent of whites over 65 and 58 percent of African Americans reported home ownership (Jackson and Wood, 1976). For many Hispanics, urban residence may also work against home ownership.

Family. Family provides another source of nonincome financial asset, along with the affective nurturing and social support they, ideally, give. They provide places in their homes for elders who are unable to live alone due to physical or cognitive impairments. In the words of Robert Frost "Home is where, when you have to go there, they have to take you in." Yet it is increasingly clear that both African American and white old people do not want to go to their children's homes as long as there are other noninstitutional alternatives (Troll, 1971, Markides et al., 1983). Respect for elders and family solidarity are historically part of Hispanic culture, but it is not clear that older Hispanic people in the United States are more willing to live with their children than whites or African Americans (Tienda and Angel, 1982).

In discussing the question of dependence on family, it must be pointed out that the great majority of older people are relatively healthy and can maintain both financial and functional independence. There is an accurate and much-quoted statistic that only 5 percent of people over 65 are in nursing homes (Brody, 1973; Fox and Clauser, 1980; Weissert and Scanlon, 1982). This is true for any given point in time, but a much larger percentage will need assistance in the routine activities of daily living (ADLs) such as bathing, eating, dressing, and toileting at some point in their remaining lifetime, and 20 percent of them will eventually be institutionalized (LaVor, 1979). Despite the media picture of the uncaring younger generation, the families of older people, as well as the older people themselves, usually try a variety of other alternatives before resorting to institutionalization. Frequently, moving in with family and institutionalization are not mutually exclusive choices, but two stages in coping with deteriorating chronic conditions. Recently a continuum of home nursing and care services has been developed as a means of trying to delay or avoid institutionalization (Weissert, 1981, 1983, 1984), but they are expensive (either to the recipient, the family, or the government) and have not yet been conclusively shown to postpone institutionalization significantly (Weissert, 1980, 1983).

Anecdotal material and descriptive works have suggested cultural differences among African Americans, whites, and Hispanics in the likelihood of older people living with relatives other than spouses. Hispanics have been portrayed as a traditional people for whom extended, multigenerational households are the norm (Staples and Mirande, 1980). Whites of different European backgrounds have had different characteristics ascribed to them, but in general they have been portrayed as less warm than Hispanics (Staples and Mirande, 1980). There are conflicting views of African Americans. One, hotly contested by Jackson (1972), is that there is a breakdown of the African American family, and that young people do not take care of their elders. The other is the picture of the African American matriarch ruling over a multigenerational household (Staples and Mirande, 1980; Tienda and Angel, 1982). Noncultural ethnic differences that might also affect living arrangements are number of children (including the incidence of childlessness) and marital disruption. Married couples can often manage to maintain an independent household even when both have chronic, serious health problems. Divorce, on the other hand, may eliminate children as sources of support for the noncustodial parent if the separation was bitter.

This research cannot discern cultural influences or family feelings. It can identify ethnic differences in living arrangements, if they exist, and it can examine whether or not they persist when family income, the existence of children, and marital status are controlled.

Government Transfers. Government programs for the poor and those specifically for older adults may affect older people of minority and majority status differently, even though there is no overt discrimination in their design. Programs may be age-based (e.g., Medicare, property tax exemptions, or extra income tax deductions), need-based (e.g., food stamps or Medicaid) or age- and need-based (e.g., Supplementary Security Income). Nelson (1983) has argued powerfully that those programs which are exclusively age-based—especially tax exemptions and deductions—disproportionately benefit the most affluent elders and are much more costly than need-based programs. Benefits from tax exemptions and deductions cannot be discerned from the data used in this study. Since these exceptions are disproportionately advantageous to the well-to-do elderly, use of data on transfer payments alone may exaggerate the leveling influence of government programs.

Because of more disadvantaged work histories (both in kinds of work and length of uninterrupted employment), African Americans have been shown to be both less likely to qualify for Social Security and less likely to have earned the highest benefits when they do qualify (Snyder, 1979). Hispanics, whose work histories fall between those of whites and African Americans, may be expected also to fall between them in pension earnings. Conversely, for much the same reasons, African Americans are more likely than whites to qualify for need-based programs, and Hispanics, again, are likely to fall between African Americans and whites. One exception is the illegal Mexican immigrant or the Mexican-American citizen who lives in a barrio where there are many illegal immigrants. He may be very hesitant to apply for needed aid out of fear for himself or general mistrust of government. Saenz (1972) asserts that distrust of government, whether in Mexico or the United States, is an historical cultural pattern of the Mexican people independent of any fear of immigration status. However, this subgroup is unlikely to appear in a census sample for the same reasons, as will be discussed in Chapter 2.

Preview of Remaining Chapters

The discussion of ethnic differences in this book will be limited to financial and demographic variables. The choice to exclude social, emotional, and spiritual support systems from this research was made from a need for conceptual clarity and an awareness of the limitations of secondary data sources. It does not reflect a lack of respect for the enrichment provided by the strong family bonds of the Hispanic community, the strength and hope provided by the church in the African American community (with apologies to Jackson [1972] who deplores this generalization), the resiliency gained from years of meeting adversity, or any other nonmaterial wealth of today's elders in any ethnic group. Neither does it assume that financial goods and well-being are synonymous. There is, however, an underlying assumption that very low income and very large losses of income are negatively valued by all but voluntary ascetics and that large, systematic differences in income among groups of people are suggestive of social injustice. These assumptions cannot but influence the interpretation of findings, and thus they are stated here explicitly as a warning to the reader.

Chapter 2 describes the data and methodology of this study. It deals with the temporal dimensions of the study and shows the strengths and weakness of these data in dealing with time. It describes data comparability, and the special problems of compatibility in the Hispanic samples. Finally, it gives a methodological preview of Chapters 3 and 4.

Chapter 3 describes empirically the ethnic income differences before the effects of aging/retirement, building on the historical overview presented in the preceding section. Data gathered at ages 55 to 64 are used to demonstrate the ethnic differences in education, occupation, labor force participation, marital status, and place of residence of those who survived into these age groups, and the relative effects on family income and poverty status of these variables.

Chapter 4 tests the relative merits of the concepts double jeopardy, parallel jeopardy, and leveling by examining the real-money differences between ethnic groups within the same cohort at four points in time. Cohort A, the oldest of the cohorts, presents the best test of these hypotheses because it furnishes data for ages 55 to 64, 65 to 74, 75 to 84, and 85 to 94 (see table 1 in Chapter 2). Data from the other cohorts point up cohort differences and help identify the influence of historical/economic changes that might either mask or exaggerate the findings.

In addition to presenting the trends that may be characterized as jeopardy or leveling, Chapter 4 shows how the variables that influenced the ethnic differences in income and poverty status at ages 55 to 64 persist, grow, or diminish as aging continues.

Chapter 5 examines the question of income from assets (such as rents and dividends) and nonincome assets (such as family living arrangements and government transfer programs) to see whether these diminish or magnify the ethnic differences revealed when family income and family poverty status are used as measures of financial well-being.

Chapter 6 summarizes the research findings of Chapters 3 through 5. Then, having identified factors that have predicted ethnic income differences among today's older adults, it looks at published census data to explore signs of greater equality among ethnic groups in today's younger cohorts. It returns to the theoretical framework presented in Chapter 1, places empirical findings in theoretical context, and finally speculates on the future of tomorrow's ethnic elders.

Notes

[1]Dowd is referring to power within the society as a whole. There are determinants of power unique to a given age or social setting. Examples include the child who is older, or a more daring athlete, and the retiree who is vigorous, active, and "youthful." It is possible that these age-specific determinants of status are of magnified importance in groups with little power vis-à-vis the whole society.

[2]The use of figures to illustrate the possible relationships between ethnic income differences and income changes that accompany aging was suggested by very similar figures in Pampel (1981).

[3]The sixth dimension, age, is omitted from consideration for this portion of the book because the focus is on differences within small age groupings.

[4]The strip of land which now constitutes the southern borders of Arizona and New Mexico, known as the Gadsden Purchase, was acquired 43 years before Cohort A was born, in 1853.

[5]Alger (1832–99) was published from the Civil War era to 1905, but his greatest popularity came in 1910 when Cohort A were 5 to 14 years old. More of Alger's books were sold in that one year than in any year in his lifetime. However, by 1920 his work had fallen from popularity (Scheinherst and Boles, 1985).

[6]The presence of people with Hispanic surnames, famous and unknown, in mainstream white America is *prima facie* evidence of the possibility of assimilation. However, many Mexican-American writers (including Samora) believe that there are racial barriers for Mexican-Americans because they are "bronze" and of racially mixed heritage.

[7]Texas and Florida. The other two are California and New York.

II
Data and Methodology

This chapter presents the procedural and methodological details of the research necessary to answer the questions posed in Chapter 1. Sections will be devoted to data, methods, operational definitions, and the generalizability of findings. Explanations of special problems encountered in this research and efforts to resolve will then be addressed.

The Data

The survey data for this study are drawn from the 1 in 1,000 state-level Public Use Samples (PUSs) of the United States Census of Population and Housing for 1960, 1970, and 1980 and the 1 percent Public Use Microdata Sample (PUMS) from the 1990 Census. Additional data describing sources of income in 1980 were obtained from the March 1980 Current Population Survey (CPS).

The PUS and the PUMS are each a sample of a sample of a sample. In each of the relevant census years, detailed data were collected for a stratified, random sample of the population—25 percent in 1960, 5 and 15 percent (different sets of questions) in 1970, and 5 percent in 1980. In 1990 a variable sampling rate was used for this question, ranging from 1 in 2 in small rural areas to 1 in 8 in some dense ones. In most places the rate was 1 in 6 or 16.7 percent (U.S. Bureau of the Census, 1972b; 1973c; 1981b 1983b, and 1992c). From this sample population data, a 1 percent stratified subsample tape was made; and from the 1 percent sample one or more stratified, systematic subsamples were drawn. For 1970, Public Use Samples were drawn from both the 15 percent and 5 percent samples. This study uses the subsample drawn from the 5 percent sample because of its greater comparability with the 1980 PUS and the Current Population Survey.

The Current Population Survey is conducted in 644 sample areas in 1,000 counties and independent cities, representing every state and the District of Columbia. It is designed to be representative of its universe—the civilian, noninstitutionalized population of the United

States. The March 1980 CPS contains 147,000 people 14 years of age and older with an extra sample of 2,500 Hispanic households. (U. S. Bureau of the Census, 1981b)

Because these are "representative" but not random samples, the statistical programs used in the analyses here slightly underestimate standard errors. However, the trends shown in the data that will be presented here are sufficiently large to inspire confidence in findings even though tests of significance use unadjusted standard errors.

The Sample

From each of these data sources were drawn records of people born between 1896 and 1925. These were then divided into three ten-year groups of birth cohorts, referred to as cohorts or cohort groups interchangeably throughout this book. Table 2-1 indicates the ages of cohort members for the time of each survey. Because the 1990 age variable truncates at 90, recording "90 or older," the last panel of cohort A includes a few people over age 94 who were not eligible for sampling at earlier points. Less than 32 percent of Cohort A was 90 or older in that sample. If we assume the average rate of attrition in the years after 89 that we observe between individual years from ages 85 to 89 (a conservative estimate since life expectancy declines rapidly in the older years), we would estimate that 0.7 percent of the sample is older than 94 (about 229 people).

Table 2-1. Ages of Cohort Members for Each Sample Point

		Year of Census			
Cohort	*Year of Birth*	*1960*	*1970*	*1980*	*1990*
A	1896–1905	55–64	65–74	75–84	85+
B	1906–1915	45–54	55–64	65–74	75–84
C	1916–1925	55–44	45–54	55–64	65–74

From these birth cohorts were selected three ethnic groups: non-Hispanic African Americans, Hispanic non–African Americans, and non-Hispanic whites. For stylistic reasons, these ethnic groups will be referred to simply as African Americans, Hispanics, and whites. The decision to exclude people who were both African American and of

Hispanic origin from the sample was based on the social/cultural ambiguity of their position and their extremely small numbers, which made separate analysis impossible.

The Question of Time: Cross-Sectional, Trend, and Cohort Analysis

The questions addressed, and to a lesser degree the data available, require the use of three different temporal approaches—cross-sectional, trend, and cohort—as appropriate in various portions of the research. Cross-sectional analysis, comparing across groups at one point in time, is used for the initial baseline assessment of ethnic differences. This includes the demonstration and analysis of ethnic income differences within one cohort at one point in time. A second example is the more detailed analysis of income sources using the 1980 Current Population Survey to study differences among age groups (represented by the three cohorts) at one point in time. Trend analysis, comparing the same age groups from two time periods, is also an essential part of the baseline analysis. Here, for example, the ethnic differences in some measures of socioeconomic status among those who were 55 to 64 in 1960 are compared with differences in the same variables among those who were 55 to 64 in 1970 and 1980. Cohort analysis, the examination of changes among the same group of people at different points in time, is used to assess the competing hypotheses of double jeopardy, parallel jeopardy, and leveling. For example, the ethnic differences in income or poverty rate among those who were 55 to 64 in 1960 are compared with differences in the same variables among those who were 65 to 74 in 1970, 75 to 84 in 1980, and 85 or older in 1990.

Comparability of Data

Whenever longitudinal data are used, whether in trend or cohort analysis, the comparability of data must be assured if results are to be meaningful. Under the general rubric of comparability are two issues: comparability of variables and comparability of samples.

In this research, comparability of samples is relatively good. All five samples are from national surveys designed by the U.S. Bureau of the Census with comparability as one of several competing priorities.

Nevertheless, there is one serious flaw in sample comparability—the changing measurement of Hispanic ethnicity between the 1960 and 1970 Censuses.

The Hispanic Sample

In the 1970, 1980, and 1990 census and the 1980 Current Population Survey, Hispanic ethnicity was self-identified from a list of nationalities and ethnic labels, e.g., Spanish, Mexican-American, Chicano, Hispanic, Puerto Rican, Latin American. This question did not appear on the 1960 Census. However, Hispanic ethnicity can be determined for part of the sample. For this research a person in the 1960 Public Use Sample is identified as Hispanic if he or she meets one or more of the following criteria: (1) being born in Mexico, Puerto Rico, or any Latin American country; (2) having one or both parents born in Mexico, Puerto Rico, or any Latin American country; or (3) reporting Spanish as mother tongue ("the language spoken most in your home when you were growing up"). Use of the mother tongue criteria makes it possible to get *some* third generation Hispanics in the sample who would otherwise be omitted. However, a group chosen by mother tongue will be much smaller and less assimilated than a group chosen from the same population on the basis of reported ethnicity (Hernandez et al., 1973).

The smaller relative size, though not the degree of assimilation, of this 1960 Hispanic sample is shown in table 2-2, which presents the sample size by ethnicity for each of the cohorts from the four Public Use Samples. While the white and African American samples in each cohort were smaller in 1970 than in 1960, reflecting attrition with aging, the Hispanic sample increased in two of the three cohorts. This could represent net in-migration, but people over 55 seem unlikely candidates for in-migration in large numbers. This means that either census *coverage* of Hispanics increased dramatically or the number of people who were *identified as Hispanic* in 1970 but not identified as Hispanic in 1960 surpassed the attrition from mortality and return migration. The 1990 sample was 10 times as large as the samples for earlier years. Thus, for example, under the old sampling method there would be approximately 82 Hispanics in Cohort A (ages 85 and older)

Table 2-2 also indicates a second problem with the Hispanic sample—small sample size in all but the most recent data. Even combining the culturally diverse peoples of Mexican, Puerto Rican, Cuban and other Latin American descent produces a sample of fewer than

200 Hispanics aged 55 to 64 in the 1960 Public Use Sample.[1] Double sampling of Hispanics in the 1980 Current Population Survey produced a comparable Hispanic sample within a smaller overall sample for the 1980 supplementary analysis of income sources.

Table 2-2. Sample Size, by Ethnicity,[a] for Three Cohorts

	Ages					
	55–64	*65–74*	*75–84*	*85–94*	*Percent Change*	
Ethnicity	*1960*	*1970*	*1980*[b]	*1990*	*1960–70*	*1970–80*
Cohort A, Born 1896 to 1905						
W	14,061	11,096	6,778	27,247	−21.1	−38.9
H	198	253	190	822	+27.8	−24.9
AA	1,225	1,117	583	2,129	− 8.8	−47.8
Cohort B, Born 1906 to 1915						
W	18,396	16,566	13,843	94,092	− 9.9	−16.4
H	276	225	432	3,030	−18.5	+92.0
AA	1,829	1,634	1,289	7,370	−10.7	−21.1
Cohort C, Born 1916 to 1925						
W	21,341	20,142	18,406	167,175	− 5.6	− 8.6
H	434	511	697	3,181	+17.7	+36.4
AA	2,303	2,065	1,882	13,983	−10.3	−18.9

Source: 1960, 1970, 1980, and 1990 Public Use Sample tapes

[a]For this and all tables, ethnic groups are represented by W=white, H=Hispanic, and AA=African American.

[b]Hispanics were oversampled in the 1980 Public Use Sample.

A final problem in studying the Hispanic population is the question of whether samples of Hispanics taken over a twenty-year period are, in fact, samples of the same population. Because there is a pattern of circular migration, legal and illegal, in parts of the Hispanic population—especially among first-generation immigrants of Mexican origin—Hispanics who remain in the United States after retirement age are probably a select group of the best assimilated and consequently those with better resources. It seems highly unlikely that there would be a substantial amount of immigration in the older age groups, given that historically this has been non-family migration with employment in the United States as the primary incentive.

The more advantaged are also more likely to have legal resident status and thus to allow themselves to be included in the census count. Combined with the mother tongue limitations discussed above, this should produce a sample in which the well-being of the first generation is overstated, while that of the third generation is understated. Mortality differentials and migration both work to select the poorest and least educated out of the sample over time, but mortality should have the same selective effect, albeit at different levels, on all three ethnic groups.

The reader is advised that the problems presented by the Hispanic group—lack of comparability among samples, small sample size, sociocultural diversity, and attrition through out-migration—represent the weakest point in this book. Some indicators of their extent can be seen in sample size, and in the change in the proportion of first generation Hispanic Americans in successive sample points within a cohort. However, they can not be eliminated. As a result, the findings for the Hispanic ethnic group will be more suggestive than definitive.

In the face of these problems there remain two strong reasons for including Hispanics in this research. First, they are an ethnic group of growing size and importance, yet a substantial portion of the gerontological literature on Hispanics remains journalistic and descriptive. Second, it is valuable to be able to separate the effects of being a member of some minority from the effects of membership in a specific minority. The different history of African Americans and Hispanics in the United States makes these two groups well-suited for this purpose, as well as intrinsically interesting.

Variable Recodes

Because conventional demographic and economic variables are of interest in this work, and because of the advantage discussed earlier in using data collected by a single agency, most of the Public Use Sample variables to be used in trend and/or cohort analysis were relatively comparable across the three points in time. The ratio of family income to the poverty level was not available for 1960.[2] Therefore, that variable is only compared among three points in time. For poverty ratio and for a few additional variables such as hours worked, recoding was necessary to make comparable categories across time, even though this resulted in slightly larger categories and thus some loss of information. In other cases, recoding was necessary because codes for ordinal data were not in entirely linear order.

The recoding described above is quite routine and mechanical. There was, however, one important variable for which categories were not arranged in hierarchical order and values were not coded at all consistently over time—occupation. The census reports three-digit, occupational codes. However, as the American labor market has changed, the numbering of these occupations, and even which occupations exist, has changed along with it. Simply grouping occupations by the first of their three digits would create incomparability across time and would combine some logically dissimilar occupations within any given year. The classification scheme which I chose eliminated farmers, farm laborers, and military personnel who cannot be comfortably placed in hierarchical relationship to other occupations without additional information (e.g., farm holdings or military rank). Remaining workers were divided into seven occupational categories: (1) upper level white collar—professional, technical, administrative, and managerial; (2) sales; (3) clerical; (4) skilled blue collar; (5) semi-skilled and unskilled blue collar; (6) service, other than household; and (7) household service. These groupings have face validity and can be accurately coded for all four Public Use Samples.[3] Like every other system of classification that attempts to group occupation into a monotonic arrangement and preserve adequate cell size, this system overgeneralizes and is not representative of the subtle nuances in occupational status. If, as expected, occupation coded in this fashion is significantly correlated with income, then it probably adequately represents the concept. Only if it shows an unexpected relationship to this variable will serious coding inadequacies be suspected.

Aside from the this conventional criticism of occupational categories, the exclusion of farm laborers, which is also a conventional solution, threatens one special problem for this study. Hispanics may disproportionately be employed in farm labor, given their traditional (perhaps stereotypic) role as migrant harvesters. On the other hand, this is a job that frequently falls to illegal immigrants who are unlikely to appear in the census sample. If this is the case, then there should be no substantial, systematic loss of Hispanics from the usable sample when occupation is coded in this manner. Table 2-3, which gives the percentage of two ethnic groups lost to multivariate analysis because of missing data on one or more variables and the proportion of the total sample missing of the occupational recoding, shows that missing data are only slightly more common among Hispanics than among African Americans and in the sample as a whole. Therefore, this coding of the occupational variable is not seriously flawed by systematically eliminating Hispanics from the sample.

Table 2-3. Percent of Hispanic and African American Respondents Missing from Multivariate Analysis: All Cohorts, 1980

	Percent with Missing Data		
Cohort	*Entire Sample Occupation Only*	*Hispanics Any Variable*	*African Americans Any Variable*
A	1.7	3.7	1.0
B	3.1	4.2	2.3
C	2.9	4.2	1.6

The independent variable, family income, was also coded inconsistently across the samples (in addition to the problem of inflation discussed later in this chapter). Personal income was recorded as family income for one-person families in 1960 and 1970, but had to be recoded into family income for people living alone or in non-family situations in 1980 and 1990. Further, all income figures in 1960 and 1970 were recorded in hundred-dollar ranges and in hundreds of dollars. Thus, an income code of 60 in the 1960 and 1970 samples represents $6,000 to 6,099. In 1980 and 1990, income was coded in single dollars so that $6,025 was coded as 6025. Income figures in 1960 and 1970 are reported as the income codes multiplied by 100, resulting in small inaccuracies of from $0 to 99 at every income level.

Comparability of Parameter Estimates

Comparing Regression Results within Cohorts Over Time

An important part of the cohort analysis in this study is the comparison of the changing (or persistent) effects of a set of variables—education, marital status, sex, occupation, labor force characteristics, and place of residence—on income and poverty status within a cohort. Samples drawn from the same cohort at three points in time represent independent samples from the same population (subject to reservations about the shifting Hispanic population described above). Therefore, a *t*-test of significance can be used to test the hypothesis that the unstandardized coefficient of an independent variable in 1960 is not equal to the unstandardized coefficient for the same independent variable in 1970, against the null hypothesis of no difference (Hanushek and Jackson, 1977).[4]

The equation for this test of differences between 1960 and 1970 is:

$$t = \frac{(b_{1960} - b_{1970})}{\sqrt{(s.e.\ \text{of}\ b_{1960})^2 + (s.e.\ \text{of}\ b_{1970})^2}}$$

where b is the unstandardized coefficient, and *s.e. of b* is the standard error of the unstandardized coefficient.

It is not possible to do a reliable t-test for the differences between parameters from 1980 to 1990. Increases in the proportions out of the labor force in 1990 for all three cohorts necessitated eliminating the variable *working less than 48 weeks in the past year* because of its high correlation with hours worked and occupation. (Occupation itself includes a category for those who have been out of work for several years and thus have no usual occupation.) Because the elimination of this variable affects the parameter estimates for the other variables, the t-test of differences would not be reliable, though it is probably safe to assume that large differences in parameter estimates for variables other than those directly related to employment mark real changes within the cohort rather than chance.

The Problem of Inflation in Longitudinal Studies of Financial Resources

Without adjustment, it is almost certain that parameter estimates that represent dollars of income, as when family income is the dependent variable, will be significantly different over time because of inflation. It is therefore necessary when comparing dollar amounts, as opposed to ratios, to convert to constant dollars. Wherever the use of constant dollars is appropriate, money amounts will be converted to 1990 equivalents. This is determined by multiplying the dollar amount in time t by the ratio of the cost of living in time t to the cost of living in 1990. Thus, 1960 dollar values are multiplied by a factor of 4.39, 1970 dollar values are multiplied by a factor of 3.37, and 1980 dollars are multiplied by a factor of 1.59.[5]

Methodological Overview

Chapter 1 introduced four research questions to be answered in Chapters 3 through 6 of this work. This chapter has provided a description of the data, the temporal approach, and the methodological problems peculiar to the research in this book. It will conclude with a brief description of the methods used to answer the specific questions posed in the remaining chapters.

Chapter 3 examines two questions: what were the differences in income and the sociodemographic characteristics that are related to income among ethnic groups when the cohorts that are now elderly were in their peak productive years? What variables help explain these differences?

The first step in answering these questions is to examine the frequency distributions of a number of income-related variables by ethnic group and, where appropriate, by sex, for some age range below 65. The 55 to 64 age range was chosen because data for those ages are available for all three cohorts and to give continuity with the post-retirement years. In 1960, but not in the other census years, that age group had the highest median family income.[6] After examining the differences in these socioeconomic variables, ethnic differences in family income are studied, comparing *median family income* (dollar amounts and ratio of African American to white, Hispanic to white, and African American to Hispanic), *family income quartile*s (also in dollar amounts and ratios among ethnic groups), and the distribution of *the ratio of family income to the poverty level.* Finally, multiple regression is used to estimate the contribution of ethnicity to family income with the array of other socioeconomic variable controlled (*education*, *sex*, *age*, *occupation*, *working 48 or more weeks in the past year*, *marital status*, *living in the South*, *rural or central city residence,* and *living arrangements*) for two equations. One uses *family income* as the dependent variable, and the other uses the same independent variables, but uses the *ratio of family income to the poverty level* as the dependent variable.

Chapter 4 examines three questions: How did the income differences among ethnic groups change as these cohorts aged? Are any of the meanings of double jeopardy supported by these differences? Did those variables that helped explain ethnic differences when the cohorts were younger gain, lose, or maintain their explanatory power as the cohorts aged?

These questions will be answered by a cohort analysis of ethnic differences in *median income*, *income quartiles*, and *ratio of family income to the poverty level*. Cohort A will be most useful in testing the double jeopardy and leveling concepts, representing as it does, the population aged 55 to 64 in 1960, 65 to 74 in 1970, 75 to 84 in 1980, and 85 to 94 in 1990. Cohort B also moves from the preretirement to postretirement years in the course of the four census dates. Cohort C only reaches ages 65 to 74 in 1980, but it provides an indication of income changes in the working ages over the period 1960 to 1980. To answer the question about the relative strength of such factors as ethnicity, education, and region as a cohort ages, the same regression equations used in Chapter 3 are estimated for all cohorts in all three time periods. Differences in parameter estimates will be tested using the *t*-test described in the preceding section.

Chapter 5 examines three questions about other types of resources. How do assets such as savings and investments contribute to inequality among ethnic groups? What is the role of political policies and government programs in perpetuating or reducing inequity? What are ethnic differences in the resource available from family assistance and living arrangements?

Attempts to answer these questions will be largely exploratory. Assets and transfer payments will both be included in the distribution of income, by source, among ethnic groups. Then, those sources which are seen to vary significantly among ethnic groups will be studied in more detail. Home ownership among ethnic groups will be examined separately, and multiple regression will be used to look at the influence of ethnicity on home ownership with income and other socioeconomic variables controlled. Finally, ethnic differences in the distribution of living arrangements are explored. For those time/cohort groupings younger than 65, the probability of having a person 65 or older in the house is examined. For those time/cohort groupings 65 and older, the probability of living with someone other than a spouse is examined—to identify both older people moving in with younger relatives and older people who are heads of households that include younger relatives.

Chapter 6 examines the question: what do the findings of this research, in light of the current trends among younger African Americans and Hispanics, suggest about the future of minority elders in the United States? This chapter is largely speculative in nature. In summarizing the results in Chapters 3 through 5, it identifies those factors which appear to have the strongest influence on ethnic income differences. To whatever extent possible, published census data comparing younger cohorts of African Americans, whites, and Hispanics on these variables are analyzed to suggest the prognosis for greater equality in future generations of older adults.

Notes

[1]Although this combined sample is not entirely homogeneous, there is justification for combining them to improve sample size. They face the same language barriers, have closer cultural similarities to each other than to any other ethnic groups, and are of similar racial background. Indeed, the common treatment they face vis-à-vis non-Hispanic whites is exemplified in the common failure to recognize that they are culturally diverse.

[2]The definition of poverty was developed by the Department of Agriculture in 1955 but officially adopted in 1961 by the Council of Economic Advisers (O'Rand, 1982).

[3]1960 Census Recodes:

Upper-level white collar ....000–195 and 250–290
Sales 380–395
Clerical....................301–370
Skilled blue collar....................401–545
Semi- and unskilled blue collar....................601–775 and 960–985
Non–household service....................810–890
Household service....................801–804

1970 Census Recodes:

Upper-level white collar 001–246
Sales....................260–296
Clerical....................301–396
Skilled blue collar....................401–575 and 586
Semi- and unskilled blue collar....................601–796
Non–household service....................901–976
Household service....................980–986

1980 and 1890 Census Recodes:

Upper-level white collar 003–235
Sales....................243–285
Clerical....................303–389
Skilled blue collar....................503–699
Semi- and unskilled blue collar....................703–899
Non–household service....................413–469

[4]Special thanks to Rachel Rosenfeld, Ph.D. for helping to translate Hanushek and Jackson.

[5]In fact, numbers reported in 1980 constant dollars in the original dissertation on which this book is based were converted directly from 1980 dollars to 1990. This resulted in some rounding error, but no more than might be expected from converting them back to the original dollars and forward to 1990 dollars. In light of the rounding differences introduced by the differences in the data points, such errors are trivial.

[6]In 1970, 1980, and 1990, the highest median family income fell to the 45 to 54 year old age group.

III
Ethnic Differences before Retirement

To assess the effects of aging on the financial well-being of ethnic groups, it is necessary to establish a baseline, a measure of where each group was before entering old age. This will serve three research purposes: (1) it will provide the benchmark against which income divergence (double jeopardy) or convergence (leveling) can be observed; (2) it will elucidate some of the mechanisms that produce ethnic inequality and how their effects may be weakened or exacerbated by aging; and (3) it will demonstrate differences among the three study cohorts that have implications for future cohorts of African Americans and Hispanics. The position of each cohort at ages 55 to 64 (occupied in 1960, 1970, and 1980 respectively) serves as the baseline for this study.

This chapter presents the ethnic differences in family income and poverty rate at ages 55 to 64, with some discussion of cohort differences. It then examines the distribution of variables that represent historical sources of inequality for African Americans and Hispanics, measured at ages 55 to 64. (See the discussion of historical context in Chapter 1.) Finally, it uses multiple regression to examine the relative contributions of these variables and the relationship between ethnicity and income/poverty controlling for these variables.

Family Income

Family income is used here as a measure of financial well-being. Individual income seriously understates the resources available, particularly for married people who constitute the majority of the middle-aged and elderly population. Although there is some loss of accuracy in comparing family income among families of different sizes, this presents a more accurate picture of income for the majority of people.[1]

Tables 3-1 through 3-3 present baseline median family income for the three study cohorts. The dollar figures in table 3-1 are *not* adjusted, but represent the currency of the years reported. The focus is on income ratios among the three groups within any given cohort. In 1960 median family income for African Americans aged 55 to 64 was only 49 percent of that for whites in the same cohort. At the same time Hispanics in Cohort A had 77 percent of the median family income of whites. For all three cohorts, Hispanic income falls between that of African Americans and whites. Among African Americans, Cohorts A and B (those who were 55 to 64 in 1970 and 1980 respectively) fared somewhat better in relation to whites, with incomes 55 percent of the white median for both cohorts.

What cohort differences in race-specific incomes account for the relative improvement in African American income between Cohort A and the younger cohorts? Table 3-2 demonstrates that both African Americans and whites in the younger cohorts have much higher real incomes than their counterparts in Cohort A. However, the race-specific income superiority of the younger cohorts is greater for African Americans than whites (e.g., at the baseline age, African Americans in Cohort B had constant-dollar incomes nearly 47 percent higher than African Americans in Cohort A, while whites in Cohort B had constant-dollar incomes only about 31 percent higher than whites in Cohort A). This suggests that younger cohorts of African Americans have experienced something closer to income equality and that this has occurred primarily through gains to African Americans rather than losses to whites.

Given the small sample size and the problems of identifying Hispanics in the 1960 sample, discussed in preceding chapters, it is somewhat difficult to interpret the trend for Hispanics. In direct contradiction to expectations, the cohort of people who were 55 to 64 in 1960, when the sample contained only first- and second-generation Hispanics and those who reported Spanish as their mother tongue, has a higher median family income relative to whites and African Americans than the other two cohorts of self-reported Hispanics. For those two cohorts whose ethnicity is self-reported, those who were 55 to 64 in 1980 (Cohort C) have higher incomes relative to both African Americans and whites than the 1970 cohort (Cohort B). The difference between Cohorts B and C may be related to the greater labor force participation of Hispanic women in the younger cohort. African American and white women had higher levels of participation in all three cohorts, but there is much less difference among cohorts. (As shown later in this chapter, male labor force participation was smaller in each successively younger cohort for all three ethnic groups.)

Table 3-1. Median Family Income, in Nominal Dollars, by Ethnicity[a] and Cohort, for the Population Aged 55 to 64

	Income			*Ratios*		
Cohort	*W*	*H*	*AA*	*AA/W*	*H/W*	*AA/H*
A (1960)	$ 5,299	$ 4,099	$ 2,599	.490	.774	.634
B (1970)	9,099	6,099	4,999	.549	.670	.820
C (1980)	19,887	15,190	10,915	.549	.764	.710

Source: Computed from Public Use Samples, 1960, 1970, 1980
[a]For this and all tables, ethnic groups are represented by W=white, H=Hispanic, and AA=African American.

Table 3-2. Median Family Income, Expressed in 1990 Dollars, by Ethnicity[a] and Cohort for the Population Aged 55 to 64

Cohort	*W*	*H*	*AA*
A (1960)	$23,435	$18,091	$11,470
B (1970)	30,628	20,530	16,826
C (1980)	31,545	24,094	17,313
Percent Increase			
Δ A to B	30.7	13.5	46.7
Δ B to C	3.0	17.3	2.9
Δ A to C	34.6	33.2	50.9

Source: Computed from Public Use Samples, 1960, 1970, 1980
[a]For this and all tables, ethnic groups are represented by W=white, H=Hispanic, and AA=African American.

Median income provides a more accurate summary of income differences than mean income, given the skewed distribution of most income variables. However, median income cannot accurately describe an unusual income distribution. For example, there is some reason to believe that the Hispanic income distribution might be bimodal because of the unusual distribution of education among Hispanics in these cohorts, described later in this chapter. Similarly, Wilson (1978) has argued that a bimodal distribution is occurring for younger cohorts of African Americans. This is caused by the simultaneous decrease in job discrimination and in the number of jobs available to people with poor skills due to past discrimination. To guard against a loss of information if such distributions should be found, income quartiles are also compared. They provide a more complete description of distribution than median income, but they are still compact enough for ready comparison, relative to deciles or larger numbers of income categories.

Table 3-3 presents the upper boundaries of income, by ethnicity, for the three cohorts. As can be seen in these tables, some African Americans and Hispanics in each cohort reach the "ceiling" income category for the census year in which they were aged 55 to 64 ($25,000+ for 1960; $50,000+ for 1970; and $75,000+ for 1980). However, both minority groups in all three cohorts show their concentration at the lower income levels in the decreasing ratio of minority to white income at each quartile boundary.

Table 3-3. Upper Boundaries of Family Income Quartiles, by Ethnicity,[a] for the Population Aged 55 to 64

				Ratios		
	W	*H*	*AA*	*AA/W*	*H/W*	*AA/H*
Cohort A						
1st	$25,000	$25,000	$25,000	1.000	1.000	1.000
2d	8,499	6,899	4,599	.541	.812	.667
3d	5,299	4,099	2,599	.490	.774	.634
4th	2,799	2,099	1,099	.393	.750	.524
Cohort B						
1st	$50,000	$50,000	$50,000	1.000	1.000	1.000
2d	14,099	10,199	8,799	.624	.723	.863
3d	9,099	6,099	4,999	.549	.670.	820
4th	5,099	3,099	2,099	.412	.608	.677
Cohort C						
1st	$75,000	$75,000	$75,000	1.000	1.000	1.000
2d	30,810	24,015	20,005	.649	.779	.833
3d	19,885	15,130	10,905	.548	.761	.721
4th	11,150	7,160	4,855	.435	.642	.678

Source: Computed from Public Use Samples, 1960, 1970, 1980

[a]For this and all tables, ethnic groups are represented by W=white, H=Hispanic, and AA=African American.

For example, the boundary that separates the top quarter of African Americans from the lower three-quarters in Cohort A is a little more than half the income (54.1 percent) that separates the top quarter of whites from the lower three-quarters. However, the boundary that separates the lowest quarter of African Americans from the higher three-quarters is just over a third of the income (39.3 percent) that separates the lowest quarter of whites from the upper three-quarters in that cohort. Although the ratio of African American to white income in the lowest quartile is larger for each younger cohort, the essential similarity among the three cohorts is demonstrated by the fact that the upper boundary of the lowest quartile for whites is higher than the median income for African Americans in all three cohorts. By the same token, the median income for whites is higher than the boundary between the third and fourth quartiles for African Americans in two of the three cohorts and quite close for the third.

The position of Hispanics varies somewhat among the three cohorts for reasons discussed above, but it remains consistently between the income of African Americans and whites in all quartiles for all cohorts. If there is an Hispanic underclass of people who are more disadvantaged than African Americans, they are either very underrepresented in the census sample (not an unlikely possibility) or too small to be discerned in a quartile distribution.

Poverty Level

Relative income level among ethnic groups is of both theoretical and policy interest. However the proportion of each ethnic group whose income falls beneath the poverty level as they age is of even more pressing concern to policymakers. Because it has already been shown that Hispanic and African American income is more heavily distributed in the lower ranges, it is to be expected that both African Americans and Hispanics will be more likely than whites of the same age to have family incomes below the poverty level. Further, of these two ethnic groups, Hispanics will be less likely than African Americans to have such inadequate incomes. Table 3-4 demonstrates this to be the case for Cohorts B and C.[2]

Ten percent of whites in Cohort B had family incomes below the poverty level when they were 55 to 64 years old. For Hispanics the number was 25 percent and for African Americans, 31 percent. The relationship among the ethnic groups in Cohort C is similar, although the proportion below poverty for each group was somewhat lower—7 percent for whites, 18 percent for Hispanics, and 27 percent for African Americans.

Table 3-4. Ratio of Family Income to Poverty Level, by Ethnicity[a] and Cohort for the Population Aged 55 to 64

	W		*H*		*AA*	
	Number	*%*	*Number*	*%*	*Number*	*%*
1970, Cohort B						
<.75	1,201	7.3	70	16.6	391	24.3
.75–.99	518	3.2	34	8.1	114	7.1
1.00–1.24	494	3.0	35	8.3	123	7.6
1.25–1.49	543	3.3	44	10.4	109	6.8
1.50–1.99	1,213	7.4	37	8.8	189	11.8
2.00+	12,397	75.7	202	47.9	682	42.4
N	16,366	100.0	422	100.0	1,608	100.0
Below Poverty	1,719	10.5	104	24.6	505	31.4
1980, Cohort C						
<.75	797	4.3	90	12.9	346	18.4
.75–.99	500	2.7	35	5.0	159	8.4
1.00–1.24	514	2.8	28	4.0	140	7.4
1.25–1.49	597	3.2	41	5.9	115	6.1
1.50–1.99	1,262	6.9	84	12.1	232	12.3
2.00+	14,736	80.1	419	60.1	890	47.3
N	18,406	100.0	697	100.0	1,882	100.0
Below Poverty	1,297	7.0	125	17.9	505	26.8

Source: Calculated from Public Use Samples, 1960, 1970, 1980

[a]For this and all tables, ethnic groups are represented by W=white, H=Hispanic, and AA=African American.

Sources of Inequality

Education

When members of Cohort A were adolescents, public high schools were not universally available, mandatory school attendance laws had not been established in every state, and the usefulness of secondary education for working-class children was in question (Johnson et al., 1969; Kett, 1977; Knight, 1922). Thus, educational levels are low for all races.

Although all levels were low, they were not equal. Since this cohort was educated before even the minimal civil-rights gains that preceded World War II, there were few educational opportunities available to African Americans and few financial benefits to be gained from education.[3] Hispanics born outside the United States and those who were in the country illegally during their youths may not have attended school at all. Those who spoke Spanish as a primary language faced education entirely or nearly entirely in English, with all the frustrations attendant on working under a burden much greater than that of one's competitors. Those who were not assimilated into general Anglo culture, even if they spoke adequate English, faced ridicule and overt discrimination in many U.S. schools.[4]

Table 3-5 shows the distribution of school years completed by Cohort A, measured in 1960. Because of differential mortality of the poorly educated, this table and comparable tables for Cohorts B and C should exaggerate the average level of education attained by these cohorts in their youth.

Not unexpectedly, table 3-5 reveals that whites have a large educational advantage over both African Americans and Hispanics. The modal category is four to eight years of elementary school for all three ethnic groups; but the median years of school completed is nearly eight years for white men and less than five years for African American and Hispanic men in Cohort A. Furthermore, the distribution of years completed for African Americans and Hispanics is quite different despite rather similar medians.

Hispanic men in Cohort A are more likely than African American men in that cohort to have attended high school (23.2 percent of Hispanic men report at least one year of high school compared to 17.1 percent of African American men); and to have graduated from high school (12.5 percent compared to 8.3 percent). However, African

American men are more likely than Hispanic men to have attended school at all (90 percent of African American men in this cohort have

Table 3-5. Education Achieved by 55- to 64-Year-Olds, by Ethnicity[a] and Sex in 1960 (Cohort A)

	W		*H*		*AA*	
Education	*%*	*Cum. %*	*%*	*Cum. %*	*%*	*Cum. %*
MEN						
5+ yrs college	2.9	2.9	1.8	1.8	1.2	1.2
4 yrs college	3.8	6.7	1.8	3.6	1.0	2.2
1–3 yrs college	6.9	13.6	2.7	6.3	2.8	5.0
HS graduate	13.5	27.1	6.2	12.5	3.3	8.3
1–3 yrs HS	16.9	44.0	10.7	23.2	8.8	17.1
1–8 yrs elem.	54.1	98.1	50.0	73.2	73.0	90.1
None/< 1 year	2.1	100.2	26.8	100.0	10.0	100.1
Median	7.8		4.5		4.8	
N	6,760		112		581	
WOMEN						
5+ yrs college	2.0	2.0	0.0	___	0.6	0.6
4 yrs college	3.4	5.4	0.0	___	2.3	2.9
1–3 yrs college	9.0	14.4	1.2	1.2	3.3	6.2
HS graduate	16.6	31.0	7.0	8.2	5.0	11.2
1–3 yrs HS	17.4	48.4	3.5	11.7	8.5	19.7
1–8 yrs elem.	49.2	97.6	61.7	73.4	74.8	94.5
None/< 1 year	2.4	100.0	26.7	100.1	5.4	99.9
Median	7.9		4.0		5.5	
N	7301		86		644	

Source: Computed from Public Use Sample 1960

[a]For this and all tables, ethnic groups are represented by W=white, H=Hispanic, and AA=African American.

one or more years of education, compared to 73.2 percent of Hispanic men). Because this sample is taken from the 1960 PUS, the Hispanic group in Cohort A consists of first- and second-generation Hispanics, and those with Spanish mother tongue. This over represents the more traditional, less assimilated element in the Hispanic community.[5] However, the distributions in Cohorts B and C, which use self-reported Hispanic status, are not inconsistent with this finding. Although they reflect improved levels of educational attainment, they *do* show much larger proportions of Hispanics than African Americans with less than one year of education.

This unusual distribution of education among Hispanics suggests the possibility that the intermediate position of Hispanics in income and poverty may reflect the averaging of two widely divided classes in the Hispanic group, although income data reported earlier in this chapter do not support such a conclusion.

Table 3-6. Education Achieved by 55- to 64-Year-Olds, by Ethnicity[a] and Sex in 1970 (Cohort B)

	W		*H*		*AA*	
Education	*%*	*Cum. %*	*%*	*Cum. %*	*%*	*Cum. %*
MEN						
5+ yrs college	4.5	4.5	2.8	2.8	1.7	1.7
4 yrs college	5.3	9.8	1.4	4.2	0.8	2.5
1–3 yrs college	8.8	18.6	3.3	7.5	3.4	5.9
HS graduate	21.6	40.2	8.5	16.0	9.6	15.5
1–3 yrs HS	21.2	61.4	12.8	28.8	15.3	30.8
1–8 yrs elem.	37.8	99.2	55.5	84.3	64.1	95.4
None/< 1 year	0.8	100.0	15.6	99.9	4.7	100.1
Median	9.5		5.7		6.6	
N	7,784		211		711	
WOMEN						
5+ yrs college	2.6	2.6	0.5	0.5	2.7	2.7
4 yrs college	4.5	7.1	1.4	1.9	1.5	4.2
1–3 yrs college	9.4	16.5	3.7	5.6	3.5	7.7
HS graduate	28.5	45.0	13.6	19.2	11.4	19.1
1–3 yrs HS	21.4	66.4	14.9	34.1	19.6	38.7
1–8 yrs elem.	32.7	99.1	49.5	83.6	58.2	96.9
None/< 1 year	0.9	100.0	16.4	100.0	3.1	100.0
Median	10.4		6.1		7.3	
N	8,782		214		863	

Source: Computed from Public Use Sample 1970

[a]For this and all tables, ethnic groups are represented by W=white, H=Hispanic, and AA=African American.

The inferior educational level of Hispanic women relative to Hispanic men also sets the Hispanic group apart from African Americans and whites. (For both of those groups women are slightly better educated than men, when measured either by median years of school completed or by percent whose level of education is high school graduation or higher.) This finding suggests the very traditional nature of the Hispanic population in this cohort and has potential implications for employment, family income (the one-income versus two-income family), living arrangements, and the impact of marital disruption.

Table 3-7. Education Achieved by 55- to 64-Year-Olds, by Ethnicity[a] and Sex in 1980 (Cohort C)

	W		*H*		*AA*	
Education	*%*	*Cum. %*	*%*	*Cum. %*	*%*	*Cum. %*
MEN						
5+ yrs college	7.7	7.7	5.3	5.3	2.3	2.3
4 yrs college	8.1	15.8	3.9	9.2	1.4	3.7
1–3 yrs college	12.2	28.0	7.4	16.6	6.4	10.1
HS graduate	32.4	60.4	13.6	30.2	18.9	29.0
1–3 yrs HS	18.6	79.0	12.8	43.0	23.0	52.0
1–8 yrs elem.	20.4	99.4	49.5	92.5	45.4	97.4
None/< 1 year	0.5	99.9	7.4	99.9	2.6	100.0
Median	12.3		8.4		9.2	
N	8,680		337		813	
WOMEN						
5+ yrs college	3.4	3.4	3.0	3.0	1.8	1.8
4 yrs college	5.6	9.0	1.1	4.1	2.6	4.4
1–3 yrs college	12.1	21.1	6.8	10.9	6.3	10.7
HS graduate	40.8	61.9	17.8	28.7	18.1	28.8
1–3 yrs HS	20.4	82.3	13.4	42.1	26.3	55.1
1–3 yrs elem.	17.4	99.7	50.8	92.9	43.0	98.1
None/< 1 year	0.4	100.1	7.1	100.0	1.8	99.9
Median	12.4		8.3		9.6	
N	9,883		366		1,087	

Source: Computed from Public Use Sample 1980

[a]For this and all tables, ethnic groups are represented by W=white, H=Hispanic, and AA=African American.

Members of each successively younger cohort were better educated than their predecessors (see tables 3-6 through 3-8). Sex- and race-specific median school years completed were about two years higher in Cohort B than Cohort A, with Hispanic males showing the smallest difference (1.2 years) and white females showing the greatest (2.5 years). Sex- and race-specific median school years completed for Cohort C were, in turn, somewhat more than two years greater than those for Cohort B. The result of these almost identical race-specific gains was to keep the ethnic differences nearly constant across the three cohorts, as demonstrated in table 3-9.

Table 3-8. Median Years of School Completed for the Population Aged 55 to 64, by Cohort, Ethnicity,[a] and Sex

	Cohort			*Differences*		
Ethnicity/Sex	*A*	*B*	*C*	*B-A*	*C-B*	*C-A*
W men	7.8	9.5	12.3	1.7	2.8	4.5
W women	7.9	10.4	12.4	2.5	2.0	4.5
H men	4.5	5.7	8.4	1.2	2.7	3.9
H women	4.0	6.1	8.3	2.1	2.2	4.3
AA men	4.8	6.6	9.2	1.8	2.6	4.4
AA women	5.5	7.3	9.6	1.8	2.3	4.1

Source: Calculated from Public Use Samples, 1960, 1970 and 1980
[a]For this and all tables, ethnic groups are represented by W=white, H=Hispanic, and AA=African American.

Table 3-9. Ethnic[a] Differences in Median Years of School Completed, by Sex and Cohort, for the Population Aged 55 to 64

	Ethnic Differences								
	W-AA			*W-H*			*AA-H*		
Sex	*A*	*B*	*C*	*A*	*B*	*C*	*A*	*B*	*C*
Men	3.0	2.9	3.1	3.3	3.8	3.9	0.3	0.9	0.8
Women	2.4	3.1	2.8	3.9	4.3	4.1	1.5	1.2	1.3

Source: Calculated from Table 3-8
[a]For this and all tables, ethnic groups are represented by W=white, H=Hispanic, and AA=African American.

Still, not all years of education are of equal value. Years that mark completion of a course of study—e.g., 12 years of public school, or four years of college—are of more value as credentials for employment than other individual school years completed. Therefore, although differences in mean years of school were about the same in all three cohorts, differences that may be culturally relevant do exist. However, interpretation of these is difficult.

The percentage of African Americans graduating from high school relative to whites is slightly larger in the younger cohorts (e.g., in Cohort A African American men are only 31 percent as likely as white men to have high school educations or better, but African American men in Cohort C are 48 percent as likely as white men to have that educational level). On the other hand, it is a greater disadvantage to be poorly educated in well-educated cohorts. Thus, the disadvantage for African American men in having only 8 percent high school graduates in Cohort A may not have been very serious because a minority (27 percent) of white men had that much education. By contrast, the disadvantage of African Americans in Cohort C in having 29 percent high school graduates may have been greater because a substantial majority (over 60 percent) of white men in that cohort were high school graduates.

Marital Disruption

Marital stability represents another financial advantage for whites, and especially for white women relative to the other two groups of women. Though marital disruption is usually an economic hardship for both sexes, the superior earning power of men means that women are usually harder hit by dissolution and more financially disadvantaged by remaining unmarried. At the same time, because of men's lower life expectancy, women are more likely to face disruption in the form of widowhood. While divorce and separation affect an equal number of men and women, a higher proportion of men remarry, and they remarry more quickly. Thus, women are more likely to have the marital status "divorced."

African Americans and whites have somewhat different practices of voluntary marital disruption. Whites tend to be "separated" for only relatively short periods of time. If they do not reconcile, they proceed to get divorced. African Americans, by contrast, often remain separated for many years with no apparent intention of reconciliation, only seeking divorce if one of the parties wishes to remarry (Cherlin, 1981).

For this reason, and because of the social similarity of the two statuses, divorced and separated people will be grouped together for both analysis and discussion.

As shown in table 3-10, whites of both sexes and all three cohorts are more likely than African Americans and Hispanics to be married with spouse present at ages 55 to 64. Differences in mortality, divorce, and remarriage explain these differences among ethnic groups.

Table 3-10. Percent in Each Marital Status among the Population Aged 55 to 64, by Sex, Ethnicity,[a] and Cohort

	Men			*Women*		
Marital Status	*W*	*H*	*AA*	*W*	*H*	*AA*
COHORT A (1960)						
Married	81.5	70.5	69.2	63.0	48.8	44.9
Widowed	4.6	9.8	9.5	21.8	34.9	35.1
Divorced/Separated	6.3	8.9	14.3	7.0	10.5	14.6
Never Married	7.6	10.7	7.1	8.3	5.8	5.4
N	6,760	112	581	7,301	86	644
COHORT B (1970)						
Married	83.3	82.0	65.5	66.1	58.9	47.6
Widowed	3.8	5.2	9.3	19.4	26.6	28.5
Divorced/Separated	6.4	8.1	18.8	7.3	11.2	16.8
Never Married	6.5	4.7	6.4	7.2	3.3	7.1
N	7,784	211	771	8,782	214	863
COHORT C (1980)						
Married	86.3	81.6	67.5	70.6	59.3	44.4
Widowed	3.0	3.9	7.5	17.0	19.4	28.6
Divorced/Separated	5.9	8.0	18.9	7.9	15.6	20.5
Never Married	4.8	6.5	6.0	4.6	5.7	6.4
N	8,680	337	813	9,883	366	1,087

Source: Computed from Public Use Samples, 1960, 1970, 1980

[a]For this and all tables, ethnic groups are represented by W=white, H=Hispanic, and AA=African American.

In Cohort A, over a third of African American and Hispanic women in the sample were already widowed at ages 55 to 64 compared to 21.8 percent of white women. The younger cohorts had both lower ethnic-specific rates and smaller differences among ethnic groups. Still, even in Cohort C, more than one and a half times as many African American women were widowed as white women in this age group.

This difference in the rate of early widowhood might work in the direction of the leveling hypothesis. The high levels of widowhood among African Americans, and among Hispanics in the two older cohorts, bring a decline in income before age 65. If whites experience higher relative levels of widowhood after age 65 because a substantial number of minority women are no longer at risk, this will work to lower the post-65 income of white women more than that of the women in minority groups.

Voluntary marital disruption in the form of divorce or separation has had a relatively small impact on whites in these three cohorts. Fewer than 8 percent of whites were divorced or separated at ages 55 to 64, regardless of cohort or sex. (The range is from 6.3 percent for white men in Cohort A to 7.9 percent for white women in Cohort C.) Higher percentages of African Americans than whites were divorced at ages 55 to 64, with Hispanics once again in the intermediate position between African Americans and whites.

Younger cohorts had higher sex- and ethnic-specific percentages of divorced members than older cohorts. Further, the difference between whites and minorities is larger in the younger cohorts. Thus, for tomorrow's elderly the decreased disadvantage of African Americans and Hispanics in widowhood may be offset by an increased disadvantage in divorce and separation.

Southern Residence

For most of the nation's history, and all of the lifetime of the three study cohorts, the South has been the poorest region of the United States. Along with a generally poor economy, many southern states have "right to work" laws that effectively cripple most attempts to organize labor in the major southern industries.[6]

African Americans have historically faced more overt discrimination in the South (Wilson, 1978) than in other regions (beyond the disadvantages of the poor southern economy) and yet have continued to live in that region disproportionately. Therefore African Americans are particularly disadvantaged by southern residence.

There are also heavy concentrations of Hispanics in the southern states of Texas and Florida, which are ranked second and fourth, respectively, among the states in their number of Hispanic residents. Between them they housed 24.8 percent of the total Hispanic population in 1970 and 26.3 percent in 1980 (U.S. Bureau of the Census, 1984, 1973a). However, Florida and Texas are prosperous states by southern standards. It may be for this reason, or because anti-Hispanic discrimination is less concentrated in the South, but there is less southern regional variation in income for Hispanics than for African Americans.

Table 3-11. Median Income, in Nominal Dollars, for Men, by Ethnicity,[a] for the United States and the Four States with Largest Hispanic Populations in 1969 and 1979

	1969 (Males 14+)			*1979 (Males 15+)*		
State	*W*	*H*	*AA*	*W*	*H*	*AA*
US	$6,772	$5,210	$4,067	$12,881	$9,078	$7,827
CA	7,471	6,054	5,331	14,078	9,354	9,104
FL	5,878	5,104	3,440	11,356	9,113	6,995
NY	7,514	5,007	5,572	13,121	8,741	8,877
TX	7,941	6,749	4,281	13,149	8,279	8,118

Source: Published data from 1970 and 1980 Census

[a]For this and all tables, ethnic groups are represented by W=white, H=Hispanic, and AA=African American.

Table 3-12. Ratios of African American to White and Hispanic to White Median Income for Males in the United States and the Four States with Largest Hispanic Populations in 1969 and 1979.

	1969		*1979*	
State	*AA/W*	*H/W*	*AA/W*	*H/W*
US	.601	.769	.608	.705
CA	.714	.810	.647	.664
FL	.585	.868	.616	.802
NY	.742	.666	.677	.666
TX	.539	.850	.617	.630

Source: Computed from Table 3-11.

Table 3-11 shows the median male income, by ethnicity, for the U.S. and the four states with the largest Hispanic populations in 1969 and 1979. Table 3-12 shows the ratio of African American to white and Hispanic to white income for these same areas. This is personal income unadjusted by age so conclusions about magnitude of differences should be interpreted cautiously. However, the greater regional disadvantage of African Americans does appear clearly in these tables. The ratio of African American to white income is smaller in the two southern states than in the two non-southern states, particularly in 1969. However, the ratio of Hispanic to white income does not follow this pattern.

Given this background on the anticipated influence of southern residence on income, what are ethnic differences in southern residence within the study cohorts? Table 3-13 demonstrates that in all three cohorts African Americans are the most likely and whites the least likely to live in the South.

Table 3-13. Percent Living in the South among the Population Aged 55 to 64, by Ethnicity[a] and Cohort

Cohort	*W*	*H*	*AA*
A (1960)	24.7	32.8	58.3
B (1970)	27.6	41.6	53.6
C (1980)	30.5	34.3	53.4

Source: Calculated from Public Use Samples, 1960, 1970, and 1980
[a]For this and all tables, ethnic groups are represented by W=white, H=Hispanic, and AA=African American.

Well over half of African Americans in all three cohorts live in that region, compared to less than a third of whites. Hispanics fall between whites and African Americans in southern residence, as in so many other variables. Over time the trend for whites and African Americans is moving in opposite directions. The so-called sunning of America is seen in the increase of 55 to 64 year old whites in the South from nearly 25 percent in 1960 to over 30 percent in 1980. This increase in southern whites is paralleled by a decrease in the percentage of southern African Americans, particularly from 1960 to 1970, when the proportion of African Americans living in the South fell from over 58 percent to less than 54 percent. Changes in the proportion of Hispanics does not show a single trend over time and may be influenced by changes in the relative growth of the cultural subgroups that are associated with enclaves in different states (e.g., Mexican Americans in Texas and Puerto Ricans in New York).

Central-City Residence

Residence in the central cities of metropolitan areas is also associated with lower economic status. The period 1960 to 1980, from which data for this study are drawn, was one that saw middle-class residents, industry, and commerce leave the city. Despite much publicized urban gentrification, suburbanization of the country was the prevailing trend.

Increasingly, those who remained in the city, outside of a few prestigious or historic areas, were those who could not afford to move out. As a result, cities were left with a population that had increasing per capita need and provided a declining tax base (Wilson, 1978). The proportion of central-city residents aged 55 to 64 in the three study cohorts is shown in table 3-14. In Cohort A, Hispanics are the group most heavily concentrated in central cities, 56.1 percent, while African Americans in Cohorts B and C have the highest central city concentration, 56.9 percent in Cohort B and 48.8 percent in Cohort C. Whites have the proportionately smallest central-city populations in all three cohorts.

Table 3-14. Population Aged 55 to 64 Living in Central Cities, by Ethnicity[a] and Cohort

	W		*H*		*AA*	
Cohort	*Number*	*%*	*Number*	*%*	*Number*	*%*
A	4,446	31.6	111	56.1	602	49.1
B	4,775	28.8	216	50.8	930	56.9
C	3,148	17.0	296	42.1	927	48.8

Source: Computed from Public Use Samples, 1960, 1970, 1980

[a]For this and all tables, ethnic groups are represented by W=white, H=Hispanic, and AA=African American.

Flight from the central city is reflected in the ethnic-specific intercohort differences among whites and Hispanics. Each successively younger cohort has a smaller percentage of its number living in central cities (31.6 percent of 55- to 64-year old whites in Cohort A, but only 28.8 percent in Cohort B and 17 percent in Cohort C live in central cities). This pattern does not hold for African Americans, who may have less choice in housing as well as other resources and opportunities.

Work Status[7]

Education, marital disruption, and place of residence (region and size of place) influence resources indirectly in the manner sketched. The remaining sources of inequality are more direct, in that they describe the actual process of earning income for most people[8]—employment status, type of employment, and employment history (weeks worked per year and hours worked per week). Since the frequency, type, and history of employment are different for men and women, the pattern for each sex will be discussed separately.

The implications of not being employed at ages 55 to 64 are not easy to sort out. Those who are "not employed" (as opposed to "unemployed," which applies only to those in the labor force) constitute four major categories of those not at work:

1. *Nonworkers*: Those who have never worked for money, or have not worked for money for most of their adult lives. This group is made up primarily of married women with adequately employed husbands.

2. *Unemployed or unemployable*: Those who need to work but are not employed (e.g., through layoff, ill health) and do not qualify for retirement income.

3. *Early retirees*: Those who accept early retirement and have some resources.

4. *Privileged early retirees*: Those who "buy" early retirement as a luxury, which reduces their income but leaves them with more than adequate resources.

The trends in percent working can be interpreted in terms of these four categories, but this is a matter of theorizing from the data—not a set of hypotheses the data necessarily support. For example, in each of the three cohorts, white men are more likely to be working between ages 55 and 64 than Hispanic or African American men (see table 3-15). From the demographic comparisons among ethnic groups presented in this chapter, it is reasonable to assume that the larger number of whites working reflects fewer whites in the "unemployed or unemployable" category. However, the sex- and ethnic-specific cohort differences are more difficult to interpret.

For example, the percentage of men who are working declines with each successively younger cohort for whites and Hispanics. Given the higher education and average income of these younger cohorts, the most likely interpretation seems to be an increasing number of the "early retirees" and the "privileged early retirees." However, the pattern for African American men is different.

A relatively small proportion of those in Cohort A are working (68.3 percent, compared to 78.6 percent of Hispanic men and 80.3 percent of white men in the same cohort). The very low family income of African Americans in that cohort suggests that this low number working may be due to a large number of African Americans in the "unemployed or unemployable" category. The larger number of African American men working in the more prosperous Cohort B reflects the better economic times of 1970 and probably the consequent reduction of those who fit the "unemployed or unemployable" classification. But how can the proportion working among African American men in Cohort C be explained?

Table 3-15. Percent Employed at Ages 55 to 64 by Sex, Ethnicity,[a] and Cohort

	Percent Employed			*Ratio*	
Cohort	*W*	*H*	*AA*	*AA/W*	*H/W*
MEN					
A (1960)	80.3	78.6	68.3	.851	.979
B (1970)	78.6	74.4	71.3	.907	.947
C (1980)	69.5	65.9	56.2	.809	.948
WOMEN					
A (1960)	33.9	17.4	39.9	1.177	.513
B (1970)	40.8	24.9	43.2	1.059	.610
C (1980)	39.4	31.4	43.3	1.099	.797

Source: Computed from Public Use Samples, 1960, 1970, 1980

[a]For this and all tables, ethnic groups are represented by W=white, H=Hispanic, and AA=African American.

This group has the smallest percent at work of any of the cohort/ethnic groups of men (only 56.2 percent). It is tempting to explain this in terms of the relatively poorer economy in 1980 (relative to 1960), yet African Americans in Cohort C have higher real (constant-dollar) incomes than those in the two older cohorts. Furthermore, African Americans in Cohort C are exactly like African Americans in Cohort B in their ratio of African American to white income (.549), despite having the lowest ratio of African American to white men working (.809 compared to .851 in Cohort A and .907 in Cohort B). This probably represents some combination of three trends: (1) the increased employment of African American women (see discussion below), (2) an increased number of African Americans in the "early retiree" and "privileged retiree" categories masking the negative economic effects of (3) a larger number of "unemployed or unemployable" in the harder labor market of 1980.

For women in these three cohorts, ethnic differences within cohorts and ethnic-specific differences among cohorts are almost the inverse of those found among the men. The poorest group has the largest number of women working in every cohort, and there is a general trend for the number working to increase with each successively younger cohort.

African American women are more likely to be working for pay than white or Hispanic women in every cohort. The large number of African American women working relative to whites can probably be explained by a smaller percentage of African American "nonworkers." African American women are less likely to be married, and if the percentage of African American men at work may be used as an indicator, those who are married are less likely to have husbands who are working.[9]

The very small number of Hispanic women working may be more readily explained by cultural expectations in the more traditional Hispanic subpopulation (see Staples and Mirande, 1980, for pros and cons of this view). The extremely small number working in Cohort A might reflect the narrower definition of Hispanic in that cohort (see Chapter 2). On the other hand the difference in Hispanic women working (relative to whites) in Cohorts A and B, with different definitions of Hispanic ethnicity, is smaller than the difference in Cohorts B and C with the same definition of Hispanic ethnicity. That is, the ratio of Hispanic to white workers in Cohort B is 18.9 percent greater than in Cohort A (.610 compared to .513) while that same ratio in Cohort C is 30.7 percent greater than that in Cohort B (.797 compared to .610).

This suggests that changes in the employment of Hispanic women may be real rather than artifactual.

Table 3-16. Percent Distribution of Occupational Category for the Population Aged 55 to 64 by Sex, Ethnicity,[a] and Cohort[b]

	Men			*Women*		
Occupation	*W*	*H*	*AA*	*W*	*H*	*AA*
COHORT A (1960)						
White Collar:						
Skilled[c]	24.1	11.2	5.6	21.0	—[d]	7.7
Sales	7.8	—[d]	1.4	12.7	—[d]	—[d]
Clerical	8.0	—[d]	2.8	23.5	—[d]	2.7
Blue Collar:						
Skilled	25.6	19.1	12.4	1.6	—[d]	—[d]
Semi- and unskilled	25.8	48.3	53.5	19.3	63.6	12.2
Service:						
Household	0.2	—[d]	1.9	6.6	—[d]	57.7
Other	8.6	13.5	22.4	15.3	—[d]	18.2
N	5,530	89	428	3,387	22	336
COHORT B (1970)						
White Collar:						
Skilled[c]	24.7	11.0	6.0	19.3	13.0	10.8
Sales	7.8	4.7	1.8	10.7	8.7	1.7
Clerical	7.4	6.4	6.3	28.5	13.0	7.3
Blue Collar:						
Skilled	25.5	20.3	12.6	2.3	—[d]	—[d]
Semi- and unskilled	25.2	39.0	49.0	17.4	38.0	14.6
Service:						
Household	—[d]	—[d]	0.8	3.7	5.4	40.3
Other	9.4	18.6	23.7	18.0	19.6	24.9
N	6,922	172	621	5,255	92	519

Table 3-16 is continued on the next page.

Table 3-16. Percent Distribution of Occupational Category for the Population Aged 55 to 64 by Sex, Ethnicity,[a] and Cohort[b] (continued)

	Men			*Women*		
Occupation	*W*	*H*	*AA*	*W*	*H*	*AA*
COHORT C (1980)						
White Collar:						
Skilled[c]	28.5	14.3	8.9	21.4	13.9	14.8
Sales	10.4	5.7	2.3	13.4	9.6	2.6
Clerical	7.9	8.2	7.5	30.4	16.3	8.8
Blue Collar:						
Skilled	23.8	15.9	16.7	2.5	4.8	3.1
Semi- and unskilled	21.2	37.6	44.1	14.0	28.3	11.7
Service:						
Household	—[d]	—[d]	—[d]	1.4	5.4	20.8
Other	8.2	18.4	19.7	16.9	21.7	38.2
N	7,305	245	598	5,502	166	649

Source: Computed from Public Use Samples, 1960, 1970, 1980

[a]For this and all tables, ethnic groups are represented by W=white, H=Hispanic, and AA=African American.

[b]Excludes Farm/farm management, former members of Armed Services, and those not in the labor force in the past year.

[c]Includes professional, technical, administrative, managerial.

[d]Excludes cells with fewer than five cases.

Type of Employment

One mark of limited occupational opportunity is extremely high concentration of workers of a given ascribed status (sex or ethnicity) in a limited number of occupations. This is most clearly seen in a more detailed set of occupational categories, but as demonstrated in table 3-16, such a pattern can be discerned in even these large groupings of occupational types. For example, nearly half of the employed Hispanic men of this age in Cohort A are working in semi-skilled or unskilled blue collar jobs, as are more than half of employed African American men in the same cohort. At the same time, only about a quarter (25.8 percent) of white men are semi-skilled or unskilled blue collar workers, another quarter are skilled blue collar workers, and nearly a quarter are in professional, technical, administrative, or managerial jobs.

Jobs that employ large numbers of women tend to fall in limited sections of the broad categories represented here. For example, 21 percent of 55- to 64-year-old white women in Cohort A are skilled white-collar workers (professional, technical, administrative, or managerial), but large numbers of these are nurses and schoolteachers rather than doctors and upper-level executives. These data do not identify that sort of gender segregation in employment.

They do identify very strong racial segregation in employment among women in Cohort A. As discussed in the preceding section, only a very small proportion of Hispanic women in Cohort A are working, but the majority of those who do (63.6 percent) are semi- and unskilled blue-collar workers. Over three-quarters of the African American women in this cohort are concentrated in service occupations, nearly 58 percent of them in household service.

Ethnic-specific cohort differences suggest mild improvements in ethnic occupational segregation over time, but changes in the economic structure may explain part of that effect. For example, the percentage of African American women in household service in Cohort C is 21 percent rather than the 58 percent in Cohort A, but a major part of that decline has been offset by an increase of African American women in non–household-service jobs. This does not account for all of the difference. The proportion of African American women in skilled white-collar jobs in Cohort C is nearly double the proportion in Cohort A (14.8 percent compared to 7.7 percent), and the percentage in clerical jobs is more than triple (8.8 percent compared to 2.7 percent). However, even in Cohort C a majority of African American women still hold service jobs.

Much the same trend is seen among the three cohorts of men. There are more African American and Hispanic men in white-collar jobs in Cohort C than Cohort A. There are also more African American men in skilled blue-collar jobs in the younger cohorts. However the majority of Hispanic and African American men are in service and unskilled blue-collar jobs in all three cohorts, while the majority of white men are in white-collar and skilled blue-collar jobs.

Periodic Unemployment and Underemployment

Because of their concentration in low-skilled jobs, minority group workers face more job disruption—that is, more layoffs or a greater likelihood of working a series of temporary jobs with unemployment between each project. Another possible pattern of underemployment is working less than full time (fewer than 40 hours per week).

Table 3-17. Percent Distribution of the Number of Weeks Worked during the Year Preceding the Census for the Population Aged 55 to 64, by Sex, Ethnicity,[a] and Cohort

	Men			*Women*		
Weeks	*W*	*H*	*AA*	*W*	*H*	*AA*
COHORT A (1960)						
None	11.7	9.8	18.6	59.8	81.4	50.5
1–26	7.6	15.2	12.1	7.3	3.5	13.2
27–49	19.7	17.9	26.8	11.5	10.4	16.0
50–52	61.0	57.1	42.5	21.4	4.7	20.3
N	6,760	112	581	7,301	86	581
COHORT B (1970)						
None	13.2	16.6	20.7	52.0	70.6	49.6
1–26	6.1	9.0	5.5	7.6	4.7	8.6
27–49	16.8	21.4	22.7	13.3	9.7	18.7
50–52	63.9	53.1	51.1	27.1	15.0	23.1
N	7,784	211	771	8,782	214	863
COHORT C (1980)						
None	22.2	29.4	37.5	54.3	63.7	52.2
1–26	6.6	6.3	6.8	6.7	5.5	6.5
27–49	12.2	19.2	13.0	10.3	10.4	12.0
50–52	59.0	45.1	42.7	28.7	20.5	29.3
N	8,680	337	813	9,883	366	1,087

Source: Public Use Samples, 1960, 1970, 1980

[a]For this and all tables, ethnic groups are represented by W=white, H=Hispanic, and AA=African American.

As can be seen in tables 3-17 and 3-18, ethnic differences in these variables are smaller and follow less consistent patterns than the differences in the other employment variables. Whites are more likely to work for the entire year (except for white women in Cohort C), but among men this is largely due to the smaller number of whites who did not work at all. Percentage distribution in the categories between zero and fifty weeks vary by cohort in no readily apparent pattern for men. Disrupted work does seem to be a factor in the lives of African

American women. Those in Cohorts A and B are less likely than white women to work 50 to 52 weeks, even though they are more likely to work for pay (i.e., less likely to be in the category "none").

In every cohort, employed African Americans are also less likely than employed whites to work full time (40 or more hours per week). This is especially true in the comparison of African American and white women. However, the differences among Hispanics and the other ethnic groups are not consistent, and are probably artifacts of sample size.

Table 3-18. Percent Distribution of the Hours Worked during the Week Preceding the Census by the Population Aged 55 to 64, by Sex, Ethnicity,[a] and Cohort

Hours	*Men*			*Women*		
Worked	*W*	*H*	*AA*	*W*	*H*	*AA*
COHORT A (1960)						
1–29	6.6	11.4	12.8	17.7	21.4	31.3
30–39	8.8	5.7	9.6	20.1	14.3	16.7
40–48	63.9	69.3	64.1	54.0	57.1	41.9
49+	20.8	13.6	13.5	8.2	7.1	10.2
N	5,243	88	384	2,403	14	246
COHORT B (1970)						
1–29	6.0	9.6	8.2	16.8	12.0	29.5
30–39	11.4	15.8	10.7	22.2	26.0	21.4
40–48	64.6	61.0	71.5	54.8	50.0	45.7
49+	18.0	13.7	9.6	6.2	12.0	3.3
N	5,900	146	522	3,488	50	359
COHORT C (1980)						
1–29	9.8	12.6	11.8	23.0	21.7	29.9
30–39	7.0	4.1	6.1	20.5	20.0	17.0
40–49	62.4	67.6	71.1	50.8	53.0	48.8
50+	20.8	15.8	10.9	5.6	5.2	4.2
N	6,032	222	457	3,894	115	471

Source: Public Use Samples, 1960, 1970, and 1980

[a]For this and all tables, ethnic groups are represented by W=white, H=Hispanic, and AA=African American.

Multivariate Analysis

Having established ethnic differences in family income and in a number of variables that have been shown to be related to income, a multiple linear regression equation can be estimated to show the contribution of each of these factors to ethnic differences, as well as the relationship between ethnicity and income that remains when all of these explanatory factors are controlled. That equation is:

Family income = β_1 x Hispanic + β_2 x African American + β_3 x Female + β_4 x Age + β_5 x South + β_6 x Low Occupational Status + β_7 x Central City + β_8 x Rural + β_9 x Education + β_{10} x Married + β_{11} x Hours Worked + β_{12} x Worked Fewer than 48 Weeks

Table 3-19 shows the unstandardized regression coefficients for that equation measured as similarly as possible for the three cohorts. These coefficients may be read as dollars of income gained or lost with a change of one unit of that variable. They are presented in the currency of the year in question as well as in 1990 dollars. The variance explained by these variables, taken together, ranges from 20 percent in Cohort A to 27 percent in Cohort C.

The most pertinent finding presented in table 3-19 is that being African American at ages 55 to 64 costs between $4,500 and $5,500 in 1990 money for all three cohorts, even with occupation, labor force participation, education, marital status, and place of residence (rural and central city) controlled. The cost, in constant dollars, is somewhat smaller for each successively younger cohort, suggesting a slight increase in equity over time.

Unlike the family income differences of African Americans, those of Hispanics are not significant when these factors are controlled. Findings about Hispanics must be interpreted cautiously for the reasons explained in Chapter 2. However, these findings *suggest* that the economic difficulties of Hispanics may be attributable to those sorts of cultural disadvantages that may be directly improved—education, occupation, labor force participation, and place of residence. For African Americans, on the other hand, while improvement in all of these areas would be useful, they would not in and of themselves restore equity.

Marital status is a large, significant predictor of family income in all three census years. Being married with a spouse present is worth additional family income of $9,000 to 16,000 in 1990 dollars. It was expected that women would have lower incomes, in part because of their greater likelihood of marital dissolution, lower labor force participation, and lower occupational status for those who do participate.

It is interesting to note that when these variables are controlled, women may have a slight financial advantage over men. The coefficient for woman is positive in all three cohorts at this age, though it is significant ($p < .001$) only for Cohort A. The difference must lie among unmarried people, since there can be no sex difference in the family incomes of married people, by definition. With labor force factors also controlled, the difference is likely to lie in the greater probability that women of this age may collect survivors' pensions from deceased spouses.

Of the labor force variables, both working fewer than 48 weeks last year and occupational status (as defined in Chapter 2) are significant in this age group for all three cohorts. Hours worked last week is a much poorer predictor, confirming the trend observed in the ethnic distribution of weeks worked and hours worked, that minorities are more likely to experience underemployment in the form of weeks lost than in reduced hours.

Age within the ten-year age groups is a significant negative predictor of income for all three cohorts, but with larger coefficients in Cohorts B and C. Since the labor force participation of the respondent is controlled, but that of his/her spouse is not, the age effect shown here might be the increased likelihood of a retired spouse. It could also represent decreased responsibility and income within the same job category.

Education is significant at this age for all three cohorts. The constant-dollar value of an additional year of education is greatest in Cohort B ($2,035 in 1990 dollars) and least in Cohort A ($1,289 in 1990 dollars.)

Two of the three variables that represent place of residence proved significant for all three cohorts. Living in the South is a predictor of lower income for each of them, but what may be a sunbelt effect appears in the relative size of the coefficients. While living in the South decreases income nearly $4,000 for Cohort A in 1960 (measured in 1990 dollars), and by over $4,700 for Cohort B in 1970 (also in 1990 dollars), the decrease for Cohort C in 1990 is only $1,760.

Table 3-19. Unstandardized Regression Coefficients for an Equation with Total Family Income as the Dependent Variable, Based on the Population Aged 55 to 64

	Cohort A (1960)			*Cohort B 1970*			*Cohort C 1980*		
Variable	*1960 Dollars*		*1990 Dollars*	*1970 Dollars*		*1990 Dollars*	*1980 Dollars*		*1990 Dollars*
Hispanic	565		2,478	23		77	–4,544		– 7,208
African American	–1,257	**	–5,513	–1,413	**	– 4,760	–2,799	**	– 4,440
Woman	195	*	855	68		229	311		493
Age[a]	– 63	**	– 276	– 160	**	– 539	– 361	*	– 573
South	– 871	**	–3,820	–1,415	**	– 4,767	–1,082	*	– 1,716
Low occupation[b]	– 178	**	– 781	– 287	**	– 967	– 602	*	– 955
Central city	284	**	1,246	77		259	471		747
Rural	– 971	**	–4,259	–2,103	**	– 7,084	–3,244	*	– 5,146
Education	294	*	1,289	604	*	2,035	1,148	*	1,821
Married	1,971	**	8,645	4,053	**	13,653	9,920	*	15,735
Hours worked	18		79	119	**	401	425	*	674
Weeks worked[c]	–1,451	**	–6,364	–1,719	**	– 5,791	–4,057	*	– 6,435
R^2		.20			.23			.27	

Source: Public Use Samples, 1960, 1970, 1980

** = $p < .001$ * = $p < .05$

[a]Single years of age within the 55 to 64 age range.

[b]Highest status coded 1; out of labor force coded 8.

[c]Worked less than 48 weeks last year (includes those out of labor force).

Table 3-20. Unstandardized Regression Coefficients for an Equation with *Ratio of Family Income to the Poverty Level* as the Dependent Variable, for the Population Aged 55 to 64

Variable	*Cohort B (1970)*	*Cohort C (1980)*
Hispanic	–0.506 *	–0.285 *
African American	–0.701 *	–0.700 *
Female	0.250 *	0.164 *
Age[a]	–0.020 *	0.002
South	–0.430 *	–0.205 *
Low Occupation[b]	–0.051 *	–0.045 *
Central City	0.099 *	–0.008
Rural	–0.249 *	–0.184 *
Education	0.062 *	0.055 *
Married	0.864 *	0.849 *
Hours Worked	0.066 *	0.034 *
Weeks Worked[c]	–0.600 *	–0.555 *
R^2	.27	.24

Source: Computed from Public Use Samples, 1960, 1970, 1980
* = p <.001
[a]Single years of age within the 55 to 64 age range.
[b]Highest status coded 1; out of labor force coded 8.
[c]Worked fewer than 48 weeks last year (includes those out of labor force).

A similar trend is seen in the detrimental effects of rural life that came with the turnaround in rural to urban migration that occurred in the 1970s. While the coefficient is negative and significant for all three cohorts, the size of the coefficient is highest for Cohort B, when measured in 1990 dollars.

Central-city residence is significant only for Cohort A (1960) when race and socioeconomic variables are controlled. This lack of significance may stem from the heterogeneous nature of the variable. All metropolises have central cities, most of them containing large concentrations of low-income Hispanics and African Americans. However, these central-city areas of small and moderate size cities would seem to differ considerably from the blighted ghettoes of some of our largest metropolitan areas. Urban gentrification (the movement of upper-middle-class people to the central city)in the 1970s and 1980s may also have added to the heterogeneity that may weaken the variable.

To examine the influences of these factors on family poverty status, rather than the full range of income, an identical equation was estimated for the dependent variable ratio of the family's income to the poverty level for a family of its size. The results are presented in table 3-20. They show that the unstandardized regression coefficient for the variable African American is around -0.7 for each cohort. This means that, for example, if a given white person had an income equal to twice the poverty level (ratio 2.0), an African American person who was identical in gender, age, place of residence, marital status, occupation, and employment variables would have an income of 2.0 - 0.7, or 1.3 times the poverty rate. This is similar to the findings in estimating the equation with family income as the dependent variable. However, the ratio of family income to poverty level for Hispanics is also significantly lower than for non-Hispanics with these variables controlled—a relationship that does not hold for the family income variable. All of the dependent variables presented are significant in 1970, and all except age and central-city residence were significant in 1980.

Summary

For these three cohorts, observed in peak adult ages before most people retire (55 to 64), there are significant income differences among whites, African Americans, and Hispanics. These are related to ethnic variations in education, occupation, marital status, weeks worked, age, family living arrangement, and living in the South. For African Americans the differences persist even when all of these variables are controlled. Income differences for Hispanics, on the other hand, are no longer significant when these variables are controlled. The two minority groups also have lower ratios of family income to poverty. The same explanatory variables are significant, except for age, but in this case both Hispanic and African American differences remain significant with the other variables controlled.

Most of the same ethnic differences are observed in all three cohorts, and the magnitude of difference is large. Still, for almost every variable, minority group members in the younger cohorts are somewhat closer to their white counterparts than are those in Cohort A. This suggests some reduction in the power of the ethnic hierarchy over time, but the size of the differences among these three cohorts is not encouraging.

Chapter 4 will explore the double jeopardy hypothesis by examining how these differences change as the cohorts age. It will also examine parameter estimates of the same regression equations applied to these age/cohort measurements, to see the changing role of explanatory variables such as education, marital status, occupation, and labor force participation.

Notes

[1]It is desirable to control for those people in the sample who are living as members of extended families with younger wage earners. However, because of this variable's close relationship with marital status, its inclusion in regression equations throughout this paper would result in multicolinearity. Because the number of people in this living arrangement is very small (see Chapter 5), exclusion of this variable to allow for inclusion of marital status and avoid multicolinearity seems justified.

[2]Although a poverty level was first defined in 1955 by the Department of Agriculture, it was not accepted by the Council of Economic Advisers until 1961, and was therefore not available as a census measure when Cohort A were aged 55 to 64.

[3]A small number of African Americans held business and professional positions within the African American communities of large cities (Wilson, 1978). However, most jobs available for African Americans were race-specific and required little education. As a result, education was not as important a predictor of African American income as of white income in the 1960s; but in the first part of the following decade the dollar return on each additional year of education increased more for African Americans than for whites (Featherman and Hauser, 1976).

[4]For a good descriptive account of the plight of Hispanic children in U.S. schools see Nava (1975).

[5]See discussion in Chapter 2.

[6]State "right to work" laws were made possible in 1947 by the passage of the Taft-Hartley Act (Gould, 1993. p.48). This occurred just as unions were beginning to gain some strength in the South.

[7]The term *work status* is used here to indicate the literal fact of holding or not holding a paying job, as opposed to the technical term *employment status,* which only applies to those in the work force.

[8]The exceptions are the small number of people who can live on the income of their assets, and the retired population who live on the indirect fruits of past employment through public and private pensions.

[9]Since the number of African American men who are not working may not be distributed equally across marital status, this is not an entirely reliable indicator of the likely employment of African American husbands.

IV
Double Jeopardy and the Jeopardy of Poverty

How do the ethnic differences in family income vary as a cohort ages? What is the reality behind the double jeopardy hypothesis? This chapter presents the core of the study. It examines trends in both family income and poverty over thirty years in the three study cohorts; and reports not only changes in these variables but changes in their predictors. Trends within each cohort are discussed separately but intercohort comparisons are also included in the discussion.

Changes in Median Family Income

Cohort A

The most complete data are available for Cohort A, which began in preretirement ages (55 to 64) in 1960, and reached ages 85 and older by 1990. Changes in median family income for this group suggest that the leveling hypothesis, rather than either of the double jeopardy hypotheses, is correct, as shown in table 4-1. In the preretirement period, the median family income for African Americans was 49 percent that of whites in the same cohort, while median family income of Hispanics was 77 percent that of whites. When this cohort moved into the young-elder years in 1970 (ages 65 to 74), the ratio rose to 55 percent for African Americans, and 81 percent for Hispanics. In the next two decades, the trend of leveling persisted in this cohort, so that by the time the people in this cohort had reached the ages 85 and older in 1990, African Americans had a median family income 70 percent of whites, and older Hispanics had a higher median than whites (1.19 percent).

The mechanism of leveling is apparent in the second part of the Cohort A section of the table (percent change). White people in Cohort A experienced substantial loss of constant-dollar family income at all three data points after ages 55 to 64, though the sharpest drop occurred at the time of average retirement. Older adults in the two other cultural groups also experienced their largest decline from pre- to postretirement but they experienced smaller proportionate declines, and even showed some possible gain in the oldest ages.

Table 4-1 Median Family Income by Ethnicity,[a] Expressed in 1990 Dollars

Date (Age)	*W*	*H*	*AA*
COHORT A		*Median Income*	
1960 (55 to 64)	$23,387	$18,091	$11,470
1970 (65 to 74)	15,802	12,775	8,740
1980 (75 to 84)	12,226	11,806	7,431
1990 (85+)	10,800	12,856	7,584
		Percent Change	
Δ 1960 to 1970	−32.4	−29.4	−23.8
Δ 1970 to 1980	−22.6	− 7.6	−15.0
Δ 1980 to 1990	−11.7	8.9	2.1
Δ 1960 to 1990	−53.8	−28.9	−33.9
		Ratio of Ethnic Incomes	
	AA/W	*H/W*	*AA/H*
1960 (55 to 64)	0.490	0.774	0.634
1970 (65 to 74)	0.553	0.808	0.684
1980 (75 to 84)	0.608	0.966	0.629
1990 (85+)	0.702	1.190	0.590
COHORT B		*Median Income*	
1960 (45 to 54)	$29,124	$19,415	$14,119
1970 (55 to 64)	30,628	20,530	16,826
1980 (65 to 74)	17,175	12,330	10,699
1990 (75 to 84)	15,500	13,200	9,149
		Percent Change	
Δ 1960 to 1970	5.2	5.7	19.2
Δ 1970 to 1980	−43.9	−39.9	−36.4
Δ 1980 to 1990	− 9.8	7.1	−14.5
Δ 1960 to 1990	−46.8	−32.0	−35.2

Table 4-1 Median Family Income by Ethnicity,[a] Expressed in 1990 Dollars (continued)

COHORT B	*Ratio of Ethnic Incomes*		
(continued)	*AA/W*	*H/W*	*AA/H*
1960 (45 to 54)	0.485	0.667	0.727
1970 (55 to 64	0.549	0.670	0.820
1980 (65 to 74)	0.623	0.718	0.868
1990 (75 to 84)	0.590	0.852	0.693
COHORT C	*Median Income*		
	W	*H*	*AA*
1960 (35 to 44)	29,567	21,176	16,325
1970 (45 to 54)	39,379	28,945	23,222
1980 (55 to 64)	31,545	24,094	17,313
1990 (65 to 74)	22,400	19,400	13,161
	Percent Change		
Δ 1960 to 1970	33.2	36.7	42.2
Δ 1970 to 1980	−19.9	−16.8	−25.4
Δ 1980 to 1990	−29.0	−19.5	−24.0
Δ 1960 to 1990	−24.2	− 8.4	−19.4
	Ratio of Ethnic Incomes		
	AA/W	*H/W*	*AA/H*
1960 (35 to 44)	0.552	0.716	0.771
1970 (45 to 54)	0.590	0.735	0.802
1980 (55 to 64)	0.549	0.764	0.719
1990 (65 to 74)	0.588	0.866	0.678

Source: Computed from Public Use Samples, 1960, 1970, 1980, 1990

[a]For this and all tables, ethnic groups are represented by W=white, H=Hispanic, and AA=African American.

Thus, in the thirty years from 1960 to 1990 (as the cohort aged from 55 to 64 to 85 and older), whites in Cohort A experienced a 54 percent decline in constant-dollar income, compared to a 34 percent net decline for African Americans and a 29 percent decline for Hispanics. Ethnic differences are particularly strong *after* the initial drop into the traditional retirement ages, with whites in this cohort experiencing a 23 percent income decline from ages 65 to 74 to ages 75 to 84 compared to an 8 percent decline for Hispanics and a 15 percent decline for African Americans. While income for whites continues to decline after age 85 (around 12 percent), African Americans showed a 2 percent, and Hispanics a 9 percent increase.[1]

Cohort B

Cohort B provides data for two preretirement and two postretirement age groups. People in this cohort, like those in Cohort A, experienced a reduction of ethnic income inequality over the traditional retirement period. They had, in fact, seen a reduction during the last decade of the work years as well. However, unlike those in Cohort A, African American seniors saw a small reduction of equality in the interval from ages 65 to 74 to ages 75 to 84. Hispanic-white differences declined at each time point.

Between 1960 and 1970, when most members of this cohort were working and the economy was favorable, all three cohorts experienced income growth. There was narrowing of ethnic differences, but in this case it was due to the slightly larger income improvement of Hispanics (5.7 percent, compared to 5.2 percent for whites) and the substantially larger increase for African Americans (19.2 percent).

As shown in the second section of the Cohort B data in table 4-1, the mechanism for greater equality in Cohort B only partially parallels that in Cohort A. The narrowing of ethic differences between 1970 and 1980 (ages 55 to 64 to ages 65 to 74), like that in Cohort A, was due to smaller decreases among minority groups as all three ethnic groups experienced income decline in the ages beyond 65. However, from ages 65 to 74 to ages 75 to 84, African Americans experienced more income decline than whites. Nevertheless, the overall net change was in the direction of leveling. It is notable that for Cohort B the income loss associated with aging from ages 55 to 64 to ages 65 to 74 is larger in all three ethnic groups than for the comparable groups in Cohort A. Cohort B had higher incomes than Cohort A at both points in time (except for Hispanics aged 65 to 74), but its superiority was much greater in the preretirement than the postretirement ages, so that the overall income loss with retirement was greater. Nonetheless, Cohort B had the highest constant-dollar income in the immediate postretirement years for both African Americans and whites.

Cohort C

Cohort C was sampled at three preretirement ages and one postretirement age during the same period, so that in the years 1960 to 1990 its members aged from the 35-to-44 age range to the immediate postretirement ages, 65 to 74. Median family income for Hispanics grew closer to that of whites over the four observation points, from 72 percent in 1960 to 87 percent in 1990. However, differences in family income for African Americans and whites, and income changes among age categories within ethnic groups were different from those in the two older cohorts. The income of African Americans, expressed as a proportion of white elders' income in this cohort, rose from 55 percent at ages 35 to 44 to 59 percent at ages 45 to 54, but then fell back to 55 percent for ages 55 to 64. Nevertheless, as this cohort moved from pre- to postretirement, the whites experienced the greatest income loss, raising the ratio back to about 59 percent, somewhat supporting the leveling hypothesis.

Table 4-2 Number in Each Employment Category for Cohorts B and C during the Preretirement Ages

	Worked < 48 Weeks		*Worked 48+ Weeks*	
Cohort/Age/Year	*Number*	*%*	*Number*	*%*
WHITE				
Cohort B, 45–54 (1960)	8,818	47.9	9578	52.1
Cohort B, 55–64 (1970)	8,551	51.6	8,015	48.4
Cohort C, 45–54 (1970)	8,199	40.7	11,943	59.3
Cohort C, 55–64 (1980)	10,165	54.8	8,398	45.2
HISPANIC				
Cohort B, 45–54 (1960)	162	58.7	114	41.3
Cohort B, 55–64 (1970)	262	61.6	163	38.4
Cohort C, 45–54 (1970)	367	51.6	344	48.4
Cohort C, 55–64 (1980)	451	64.2	252	35.8
AFRICAN AMERICAN				
Cohort B, 45–54 (1960)	1,044	57.1	785	42.9
Cohort B, 55–64 (1970)	938	57.4	696	42.6
Cohort C, 45–54 (1970)	963	46.6	1,102	53.4
Cohort C, 55–64 (1980)	1,164	61.3	736	3.87

Source: Computed from Public Use Samples, 1960, 1970, 1980

Table 4-3. Median Family Income in 1990 Dollars by "Layoff" for Cohorts B and C

	White		*Hispanic*		*African American*	
Age/Cohort/Year	*Worked < 48 Weeks*	*Worked 48+ Weeks*	*Worked < 48 Weeks*	*Worked 48+ Weeks*	*Worked < 48 Weeks*	*Worked 48+ Weeks*
Ages 45–54						
Cohort B (1960)	$24,954	$32,450	$16,576	$24,072	$11,284	$17,458
Cohort C (1970)	33,826	42,905	21,720	34,498	16,339	28,445
Ages 55–64						
Cohort B (1970)	24,074	36,852	15,667	30,463	11,295	23,401
Cohort C (1980)	24,757	38,881	19,182	32,615	11,852	26,486

Ratios

	African American/White		*Hispanic/White*		*African American/Hispanic*	
Age/Cohort/Year	*Worked <48 Weeks*	*Worked 48+ Weeks*	*Worked <48 Weeks*	*Worked 48+ Weeks*	*Worked <48 Weeks*	*Worked 48+ Weeks*
Ages 45–54						
Cohort B (1960)	0.452	0.538	0.664	0.742	0.681	0.725
Cohort C (1970)	0.483	0.663	0.642	0.804	0.752	0.825
Ages 55–64						
Cohort B (1970)	0.469	0.635	0.651	0.827	0.721	0.768
Cohort C (1980)	0.479	0.681	0.775	0.840	0.618	0.811

Source: Computed from Public Use Samples, 1960, 1970, and 1980

At both preretirement age points, Cohort C had higher median incomes than Cohort B for all three ethnic groups, yet Cohort C experienced income decline between ages 45 to 54 and ages 55 to 64 while Cohort B experienced its highest median income at ages 55 to 64. This cohort difference is particularly great for African Americans. While African Americans in Cohort B had a 19 percent increase between ages 45 to 54 and 55 to 64 (the largest increase among the three ethnic groups), African Americans in Cohort C had a 25 percent decrease between ages 45 to 54 and 55 to 64 (the largest decrease among the three ethnic groups).

Some clues to the changing pattern of peak income between Cohorts B and C can be found by examining the income trends for the fully employed separately from those who did not work for all or part of the preceding year. Table 4-2 shows the proportion in each employment category for these two cohorts at the relevant points in time, and table 4-3 shows median income for the relevant times within each employment category. There are some serious limitations in this approach. Employment data are available only for the respondent and not for the respondent's spouse or other potential breadwinners in the household such as adult children or grandchildren. Therefore, a family in which no one is working full time cannot show up in the fully employed (worked 48+ weeks) category, and a family in which both the respondent and spouse are working cannot be placed in the "layoff" category (worked less than 48 weeks). However, a family with one working spouse and one retired one will be classed according to which spouse's record is being read.

Table 4-4. Percent Change in Median Family Income from Ages 45 to 54 to Ages 55 to 64, by Ethnicity, Cohort, and Layoff Status

Category	*Cohort B*	*Cohort C*
White, < 48 weeks	– 3.5	–26.6
White, 48+ weeks	13.6	– 9.4
Hispanic, < 48 weeks	– 5.5	–11.7
Hispanic, 48+ weeks	26.5	– 5.4
African American, < 48 weeks	0.1	–27.5
African Americans, 48+ weeks	34.0	– 6.9

Source: Computed from Public Use Samples, 1960, 1970, 1980

Despite these limitations, tables 4-2 through 4-4 suggest three changes that produced the different timing of the family income peak for the two younger cohorts—greater changes in the proportion employed for the whole year in Cohort C; greater losses in real income for those who were not employed for the whole year in Cohort C; and declining real income for the fully employed in Cohort C, compared to increasing real income for the fully employed in Cohort B.

Cohort C experienced a much larger decline in the percentage of people employed for the whole year (48 or more weeks) between ages 45 to 54 and ages 55 to 64 than Cohort B. This greater decline was due to both larger percentages working a whole year at the younger age period and smaller percentages working a whole year at the older age period. For example, in 1960, 42.9 percent of African Americans in Cohort B reported working 48 or more weeks in 1959, when they were 44 to 53. Ten years later 42.6 percent reported that same level of employment. However in 1970, 53.4 percent of African Americans in Cohort C reported working 48 or more weeks in 1969 when they were 44 to 53, but ten years later only 38.7 percent reported that same level of employment. The pattern was similar for the other two groups.

Income patterns within these two broad employment categories (worked < 48 weeks and worked 48+ weeks) were also different when Cohorts B and C moved through these ages. Cohort C had higher income at both ages, but for Cohort B, those who worked a full year at both census points experienced real income increase that was largest for African Americans (34 percent) and smallest for whites (13.6 percent). By contrast, those in Cohort C who were fully employed (48+ weeks) did 5 to 10 percent worse in 1980 (ages 55 to 64) than in 1970 (ages 45 to 54). Those in Cohort B who worked less than 48 weeks did slightly worse at ages 55 to 64 than at ages 45 to 54 (except for African Americans, who fared the worst of the three groups overall but about the same in each of the time periods), while those in Cohort C who were not fully employed had much larger real income declines, ranging from 12 percent for Hispanics to 28 percent for African Americans.

Changes in Income Quartiles

Cohort A

As demonstrated in the baseline data presented in Chapter 3, income quartiles present a more complete picture of income distribution than median income alone. However, as shown in table 4-5, which presents the upper boundaries of family income quartiles for Cohort A in 1960, 1970, 1980, and 1990, these data also support the leveling hypothesis. As described earlier, the highest income quartile has an artificial ceiling imposed by the original coding of the census data. However, within each of the three remaining quartiles, the ratio of African Americans' income to that of whites improved from ages 55 to 64 to ages 65 to 74, from ages 65 to 74 to ages 75 to 84, and again from ages 75 to 84 to those 85 and older.

The lowest (fourth) quartile presents the most striking example of this. In 1960, when the members of Cohort A were 55 to 64, the family income level that divided the lowest quarter of the African Americans in that cohort from the remaining three-quarters was less than 40 percent of the corresponding family income level for whites. In 1970, when the cohort was 65 to 74, the constant-dollar incomes of both ethnic groups had declined. Then the upper boundary of the fourth quartile of African American family income was 54 percent that of whites. By 1980, when the cohort was 75 to 84, there had been an additional decline in the income of the lowest quartiles; but the decline for African Americans in these ages was so small that the African American family income at the upper boundary of the fourth quartile was 67 percent that of whites. In the years from 1980 to 1990, the lowest quartile of whites saw an additional decline, while there was a small increase for African Americans in this and all of the other quartiles. Thus, the ratio of African Americans' income levels to those of whites rose to 79 percent for this oldest group. The pattern is similar for the second and third quartiles in this cohort.

Comparing Hispanics to whites also supports the leveling hypothesis, but here the changes in all quartiles do not follow the entirely consistent pattern seen in the comparison of African Americans to whites. As always, when there is something unusual about this Hispanic sample, there is some concern as to whether it reflects a population difference or is merely an artifact of problems in the sample. It is always likely that fluctuations are greater in the Hispanic group because of smaller sample size in the three early time periods and the dramatically larger sample in 1990. However, in this case the additional concern of defining Hispanics differently (discussed in Chapter 2) does not seem to be warranted. The change in definition came between 1960 and 1970, but here the relationship between Hispanic and white income is very much like that between African American and white income. As the cohort moved from ages 55 to 64 to ages 65 to 74, income declined more rapidly for whites than for Hispanics, so that in the two middle quartiles (2 and 3) the ratio of Hispanic to white income rose. The one exception is the lowest quartile, where the income for whites and Hispanics declines in identical proportions (34.7 percent), so that the ratio of Hispanic to white income in the lowest quartile remained the same in 1960 and 1970 (.750). This is not the sort of pattern disruption to be expected from substantial differences in the composition of the Hispanic sample.

It was after 1970, as the cohort aged from 65 to 74 to 75 to 84, and then to 85 and older, when the Hispanic sample was identified by the same criteria (self-report), that the pattern was disrupted. There is not only income leveling but income crossover. That is, in both the second and fourth quartile, the upper quartile boundary for 1980, and in all relevant quartiles for 1990 (second, third, and fourth), Hispanic family income was higher than the boundary for the corresponding white quartiles. Further, this crossover is not caused entirely by the decline in white income, but by increases in the boundaries of Hispanic income quartiles. While the upper boundary of the lowest constant-dollar income quartile for whites fell 20 percent as that group aged from 65 to 74 to 75 to 84, the upper boundary of the equivalent Hispanic quartile increased 7.8 percent. It is possible that this increase reflects a particularly strong financial selection through mortality and return migration, but a more likely explanation lies in ethnic differences in living arrangements. This Hispanic cohort reached old, old age with a surplus of widowed women who were much less likely to have been employed outside the home in their late middle age than either African American or white women of their cohort. Their most likely means of increasing family income was to redefine their family unit by moving in with one or more younger, wage-earning family members. The plausibility of this explanation will be explored in Chapter 5.

Table 4-5. Quartile Distribution of Family Income, in 1980 Dollars, by Ethnicity,[a] for Cohort A

	Family Income			*Ratio*		
	W	*H*	*AA*	*AA/W*	*H/W*	*AA/H*
1960						
1st	$110,336	$110,336	$110,336	1.000	1.000	1.000
2d	37,510	30,449	20,297	0.541	0.812	0.667
3d	23,387	18,091	11,470	0.490	0.774	0.634
4th	12,353	9,263	4,851	0.393	0.750	0.524
1970						
1st	$168,304	$168,304	$168,304	1.000	1.000	1.000
2d	30,934	25,890	18,156	0.587	0.837	0.701
3d	15,802	12,775	8,740	0.553	0.808	0.684
4th	8,067	6,050	4,368	0.541	0.750	0.722
1980						
1st	118,965	118,965	82,522	0.694	1.000	0.694
2d	23,706	26,553	15,148	0.639	1.120	0.570
3d	12,222	11,770	7,392	0.605	0.963	0.628
4th	6,456	6,519	4,314	0.668	1.010	0.662
1990						
1st	366,461	223,035	282,809	0.772	0.609	1.268
2d	24,039	29,195	16,564	0.689	1.214	0.567
3d	10,800	12,856	7,584	0.702	1.190	0.590
4th	5,840	6,500	4,632	0.793	1.113	0.713

Source: Computed from Public Use Samples, 1960, 1970, 1980, 1990

[a]For this and all tables, ethnic groups are represented by W=white, H=Hispanic, and AA=African American.

Cohort B

The relationship between white and African American family income quartiles in Cohort B is very similar to that in Cohort A (see tables 4-6 and 4-7). Even in the period from 1960 to 1970, when this cohort was still largely in the labor force (45-54 to 55 to 64), some income leveling occurred, suggesting that there were both historical and aging effects on relative income. In this period, income rose for each quartile of African Americans, and all but the lowest quartile of whites, but income rose faster for African Americans than for whites.

Setting aside the artificially created first quartile, the upper boundary of the second family income quartile for whites increased 12 percent, compared to a 29 percent increase for African Americans. In the third quartile, whose upper boundary is the median income of the group, the increase from 1960 to 1970 was 5 percent for whites and 19 percent for African Americans. Finally, in the lowest quartile, while the poorest whites grew poorer with an income decline of 7 percent, the line of demarcation for the poorest quarter of African Americans increased almost 7 percent.

All quartiles of whites and African Americans experienced real income decline in moving from ages 55 to 64 to ages 65 to 74 (1970 to 1980), but the proportional declines were smaller for African Americans, once again demonstrating ethnic leveling through the mechanism of relative income decline. In this cohort, the Hispanic experience paralleled that of African Americans, but at a level of income that remained intermediate between the two comparison groups.

From 1980 to 1990, the changes fit the pattern less perfectly. Both African Americans and whites continued to lose income as they aged from early to middle retirement years. However, only the poorest African Americans (the fourth quartile) saw additional leveling. The top income for this group rose from 54 percent to 62 percent of that of whites in the same cohort. At the same time, the second and third cohorts saw greater declines for African Americans than whites. Nonetheless, the net change from 1960 to 1990 was a greater decline for whites in all quartiles (except the noncomparable first) than for African Americans, lending overall support to the leveling hypothesis. Hispanic income showed an increase for all quartiles during this period. If this is not an artifact of the larger sample size, it also supports the leveling hypothesis.

Cohort C

An examination of the relative income of African Americans and whites in Cohort C (see tables 4-8 and 4-9) makes it clear that the leveling of income that occurred in the two older cohorts between 1970 and 1980 was a factor of aging/retirement and not of historical improvement in ethnic income equality. In this cohort, which moved from early- to late-middle-age from 1960 to 1980, the gap between African American and white income narrowed during the prosperous period 1970 and widened again in 1980. This was true not only of the median income, as discussed above (which corresponds to the upper limit of the third cohort), but of both other relevant quartiles as well. However, for the second and fourth quartiles, the increased inequality from 1970 to 1980 did not reach the level at which it had stood in 1960, while the median income for African Americans in this cohort in 1980 was actually a smaller proportion of median white income than it had been in 1960, when the civil rights movement was in its infancy. The lowest quartile of African Americans experienced real net income decline from 1960 to 1980, but there was a somewhat larger net decline for whites (12.7 percent for African Americans, compared to 16.5 percent for whites) so that the amount of income inequality in this quartile showed a small net decline.

Table 4-6. Percent Change in Quartile Distribution of Family Income for Cohort A

Quartile	*1960 to 1970*	*1970 to 1980*	*1980 to 1990*	*1960 to 1990*
White				
1st	52.5	–29.3	208.0	232.1
2d	–17.5	–23.4	1.4	– 35.9
3d	–32.4	–22.7	– 11.6	– 53.8
4th	–34.7	–20.0	– 9.5	– 52.7
Hispanic				
1st	52.5	–29.3	87.5	102.1
2d	–15.0	2.6	9.9	– 4.1
3d	–29.4	– 7.9	9.2	– 28.9
4th	–34.7	7.8	– 0.3	– 29.8
African American				
1st	52.5	–51.0	242.7	156.3
2d	–10.6	–16.6	9.3	– 18.4
3d	–23.8	–15.4	2.6	– 33.9
4th	– 9.9	– 1.2	7.4	– 4.5

Source: Computed from table 4-5

Among those who were employed 48 weeks or more, those in Cohort B showed universal income increases from ages 45 to 54 to ages 55 to 64, while those in Cohort C showed equally universal decline. There were ethnic fluctuations in loss, but these formed no consistent or readily interpretable pattern.

Then, as Cohort C aged into the retirement years (from 1980 to 1990), the classic leveling pattern emerged. Each of the three relevant quartiles saw a narrowing of ethnic inequality, reflecting greater losses for whites than for African Americans or Hispanics.

Table 4-7. Quartile Distribution of Family Income, in 1990 Dollars, by Ethnicity,[a] for Cohort B

	Family Income			*Ratio*		
	W	*H*	*AA*	*AA/W*	*H/W*	*AA/H*
1960						
1st	$110,336	$110,336	$110,336	1.000	1.000	1.000
2d	42,364	30,890	22,946	0.542	0.729	0.743
3d	29,124	19,415	14,119	0.485	0.667	0.727
4th	18,532	10,588	6,616	0.357	0.571	0.625
1970						
1st	168,304	168,304	168,304	1.000	1.000	1.000
2d	47,458	34,330	29,618	0.624	0.723	0.863
3d	30,628	20,530	16,826	0.549	0.670	0.820
4th	17,164	10,431	7,065	0.412	0.608	0.677
1980						
1st	118,965	118,965	118,965	1.000	1.000	1.000
2d	30,379	24,510	20,855	0.687	0.807	0.851
3d	17,175	12,328	10,699	0.623	0.718	0.868
4th	9,863	7,146	5,349	0.542	0.725	0.749
1990						
1st	580,786	396,857	329,538	0.567	0.683	0.830
2d	29,104	28,600	18,272	0.628	0.983	0.639
3d	15,500	13,200	9,149	0.590	0.852	0.693
4th	8,079	6,824	5,018	0.621	0.845	0.735

Source: Computed from Public Use Samples, 1960, 1970, 1980, 1990
[a]For this and all tables, ethnic groups are represented by W=white, H=Hispanic, and AA=African American.

Quartile differences within employment categories (worked 48 weeks or more versus worked less than 48 weeks) amplify the differences demonstrated in median income in the preretirement years (see tables 4-11 and 4-12).

For those in Cohort B who worked less than 48 weeks, the upper half in all three ethnic groups showed real income increases from ages

45 to 54 to ages 55 to 64, and both lower quartiles showed relatively modest declines. Ten years later in Cohort C, those who worked less than 48 weeks at ages 55 to 64 made substantially less than their counterparts at ages 45 to 54, and this held true for all four quartiles and all three ethnic groups.

Table 4-8. Percent Change in Quartile Distribution of Family Income for Cohort B

Quartile	*1960 to 1970*	*1970 to 1980*	*1980 to 1990*	*1960 to 1990*
White				
1st	52.5	−29.3	388.2	426.4
2d	12.0	−36.0	− 4.2	− 31.3
3d	5.2	−43.9	− 9.8	− 46.8
4th	− 7.4	−42.5	− 18.1	− 56.4
Hispanic				
1st	52.5	−29.3	233.6	259.7
2d	11.1	−28.6	16.7	− 7.4
3d	5.7	−40.0	7.1	− 32.0
4th	− 1.5	−31.5	− 4.5	− 35.5
African American				
1st	52.5	−29.3	177.0	198.7
2d	29.1	−29.6	− 12.4	− 20.4
3d	19.2	−36.4	− 14.5	− 35.2
4th	6.8	−24.3	− 6.2	− 24.2

Source: Computed from table 4-7

Table 4-9. Quartile Distribution of Family Income, in 1990 Dollars, by Ethnicity,[a] for Cohort C

	Family Income			*Ratio*		
	W	*H*	*AA*	*AA/W*	*H/W*	*AA/H*
1960						
1st	$110,336	$110,336	$110,336	1.000	1.000	1.000
2d	41,041	31,331	25,152	0.613	0.763	0.803
3d	29,565	21,181	16,325	0.552	0.716	0.771
4th	21,181	13,678	8,822	0.417	0.646	0.645

Table 4-9 is continued on the next page.

Table 4-9. Quartile Distribution of Family Income, in 1990 Dollars, by Ethnicity,[a] for Cohort C (continued)

	Family Income			*Ratio*		
	W	*H*	*AA*	*AA/W*	*H/W*	*AA/H*
1970						
1st	168,304	168,304	168,304	1.000	1.000	1.000
2d	56,210	44,092	37,360	0.665	0.784	0.847
3d	39,379	28,945	23,222	0.590	0.735	0.802
4th	26,252	16,826	12,114	0.461	0.641	0.720
1980						
1st	118,965	118,965	118,965	1.000	1.000	1.000
2d	48,871	38,093	31,732	0.649	0.779	0.833
3d	31,542	23,999	17,298	0.548	0.761	0.721
4th	17,686	11,357	7,701	0.435	0.642	0.678
1990						
1st	634,610	447,967	378,327	0.596	0.706	0.845
2d	37,823	34,500	26,000	0.687	0.912	0.754
3d	22,400	19,400	13,161	0.588	0.866	0.678
4th	12,600	9,418	6,490	0.515	0.747	0.689

Source: Computed from Public Use Samples, 1960, 1970, 1980, 1990

[a]For this and all tables, ethnic groups are represented by W=white, H=Hispanic, and AA=African American.

The Jeopardy of Poverty[2]

Because of the absence of poverty data for 1960 (detailed in Chapter 2), the data used in this study show aging from preretirement to postretirement years in only two cohorts, B and C. Therefore, the hypothesis that aging puts minorities at greater risk of poverty, which was labeled the jeopardy of poverty hypothesis in Chapter 1, can only be examined for those cohorts. Cohort A data, representing three postretirement age groups, are provided for comparison.

Although the leveling hypothesis was supported by trends in overall income, data in table 4-13 give no such clear support either to leveling or to the jeopardy of poverty. In fact, it appears to differ by cohort.

Table 4-10. Percent Change in Quartile Distribution of Family Income by Ethnicity, for Cohort C

Quartile	*1960 to 1970*	*1970 to 1980*	*1980 to 1990*	*1960 to 1990*
White				
1st	52.5	−29.3	433.4	475.2
2d	37.0	−13.1	− 22.6	− 7.8
3d	33.2	−19.9	− 29.0	− 24.2
4th	23.9	−32.6	− 28.8	− 40.5
Hispanic				
1st	52.5	−29.3	276.6	306.0
2d	40.7	−13.6	− 9.4	10.1
3d	36.7	−17.1	− 19.2	− 8.4
4th	23.0	−32.5	− 17.1	− 31.1
African American				
1st	52.5	−29.3	218.0	242.9
2d	48.5	−15.1	− 18.1	3.4
3d	42.2	−25.5	− 23.9	− 19.4
4th	37.3	−36.4	− 15.7	− 26.4

Source: Computed from table 4-9

Table 4-11. Quartile Distribution of Family Income, in 1990 Dollars, by Ethnicity,[a] for the Population in Cohorts B and C That Worked Fewer than 48 Weeks in the Preceding Year

	Family Income			*Ratio*		
Quartile	*W*	*H*	*AA*	*AA/W*	*H/W*	*AA/H*
COHORT B						
1960 (Ages 45 to 54)						
1st	$110,241	$110,241	$110,241	1.000	1.000	1.000
2d	38,624	27,335	20,103	0.520	0.708	0.735
3d	24,954	16,576	11,284	0.452	0.664	0.681
4th	13,930	8,638	4,670	0.335	0.620	0.541
1970 (Ages 55 to 64)						
1st	168,137	168,137	163,426	0.972	1.000	0.972
2d	39,879	29,790	23,737	0.595	0.747	0.797
3d	24,074	15,667	11,295	0.469	0.651	0.721
4th	11,295	7,933	4,570	0.405	0.702	0.576

Table 4-11. Quartile Distribution of Family Income, in 1990 Dollars, by Ethnicity,[a] for the Population in Cohorts B and C That Worked Fewer than 48 Weeks in the Preceding Year (continued)

Quartile	*W*	*H*	*AA*	*AA/W*	*H/W*	*AA/H*
Percent Change 1960 to 1970						
1st	52.5	52.5	48.2			
2d	3.2	9.0	18.1			
3d	− 3.5	− 5.5	0.1			
4th	−18.9	− 8.2	− 2.1			
COHORT C						
1970 (Ages 45 to 54)						
1st	$168,137	$168,137	$168,137	1.000	1.000	1.000
2d	49,967	36,852	30,127	0.603	0.738	0.818
3d	33,826	21,720	16,339	0.483	0.642	0.752
4th	20,038	10,959	7,596	0.379	0.547	0.693
1980 (Ages 55 to 64)						
1st	118,965	106,371	118,965	1.000	0.894	1.118
2d	40,408	32,427	24,313	0.602	0.802	0.750
3d	24,757	19,182	11,852	0.479	0.775	0.618
4th	12,880	9,240	5,469	0.425	0.717	0.592
Percent Change 1970 to 1980						
1st	−29.2	−36.7	−29.2			
2d	−19.1	−12.0	−19.3			
3d	−26.8	−11.7	−27.5			
4th	−35.7	−15.7	−28.0			

Source: Public Use Samples 1960, 1970, 1980

[a]For this and all tables, ethnic groups are represented by W=white, H=Hispanic, and AA=African American.

As Cohort B moves from the preretirement to immediate post-retirement years, the proportion in poverty among African Americans and Hispanics grows relatively worse. African Americans in this cohort were more than two and a half times as likely as whites to be poor at ages 55 to 64, but they were over three times as likely to be poor at ages 65 to 74; a similar pattern occurs among Hispanics. Although whites in this cohort experience a greater relative increase in poverty over the next ten-year period, so that the ratios of African

American to white poverty rates and Hispanic to white poverty rates drop from their high at ages 65 to 74, they remain higher than the ratios before retirement age for this cohort. Thus, Cohort B's experience seems to support the jeopardy of poverty hypothesis.

Table 4-12. Quartile Distribution of Family Income, in 1990 Dollars, by Ethnicity,[a] for the Population in Cohorts B and C That Worked 48 Weeks or More in the Preceding Year

	Family Income			*Ratio*		
Quartile	*W*	*H*	*AA*	*AA/W*	*H/W*	*AA/H*
COHORT B						
1960 (Ages 45 to 54)						
1st	$110,241	$110,241	$110,241	1.000	1.000	1.000
2d	45,414	35,537	25,395	0.559	0.783	0.715
3d	32,450	24,072	17,458	0.538	0.742	0.725
4th	21,867	16,576	9,520	0.435	0.758	0.574
1970 (Ages 55 to 64)						
1st	$168,137	$168,137	$168,137	1.000	1.000	1.000
2d	52,993	42,367	36,180	0.683	0.799	0.854
3d	36,852	30,463	23,401	0.635	0.827	0.768
4th	24,074	16,676	12,977	0.539	0.693	0.778
Percent Change 1960 to 1970						
1st	52.5	52.5	52.5			
2d	16.7	19.2	42.5			
3d	13.6	26.5	34.0			
4th	10.1	0.6	36.3			
COHORT C						
1970 (Ages 45 to 54)						
1st	$168,137	$168,137	$168,137	1.000	1.000	1.000
2d	59,046	51,111	42,905	0.727	0.866	0.839
3d	42,905	34,498	28,445	0.663	0.804	0.825
4th	30,127	23,737	17,348	0.576	0.788	0.731
1980 (Ages 55 to 64)						
1st	118,965	118,965	118,965	1.000	1.000	1.000
2d	56,592	45,556	40,853	0.722	0.805	0.897
3d	38,881	32,647	26,486	0.681	0.840	0.811
4th	25,471	19,526	15,557	0.611	0.767	0.797

Table 4-12 is continued on the next page.

Table 4-12. Quartile Distribution of Family Income, in 1990 Dollars, by Ethnicity,[a] for the Population in Cohorts B and C That Worked 48 Weeks or More in the Preceding Year (continued)

	Family Income			*Ratio*		
Quartile	*W*	*H*	*AA*	*AA/W*	*H/W*	*AA/H*
Percent Change 1970 to 1980						
1st	−29.2	−29.2	−29.2			
2d	− 4.2	−10.9	− 4.8			
3d	− 9.4	− 5.4	− 6.9			
4th	−15.5	−17.7	−10.3			

Source: Public Use Samples 1960, 1970, 1980
[a]For this and all tables, ethnic groups are represented by W=white, H=Hispanic, and AA=African American.

Table 4-13. Percent below Poverty by Ethnicity[a] and Cohort

	Percent below Poverty			*Ratio*		
Ages	*W*	*H*	*AA*	*AA/W*	*H/W*	*AA/H*
Cohort A						
65 to 74	20.9	36.6	47.6	2.278	1.751	1.301
75 to 84	15.8	27.0	39.0	2.468	1.709	1.444
85+	18.8	27.7	40.5	2.154	1.473	1.462
Cohort B						
55 to 64	10.5	17.9	26.8	2.552	1.705	1.497
65 to 74	10.2	22.8	32.5	3.186	2.235	1.425
75 to 84	14.0	28.4	37.7	2.693	2.029	1.327
Cohort C						
45 to 54	5.5	16.8	23.4	4.255	3.055	1.393
55 to 64	7.0	17.9	26.8	3.829	2.557	1.497
65 to 74	8.4	19.7	29.2	3.476	2.345	1.482

Source: Computed from Public Use Samples, 1960, 1970, 1980, 1990
[a]For this and all tables, ethnic groups are represented by W=white, H=Hispanic, and AA=African American.

Cohort C, by contrast, shows a decline in the ratio of minority to white poverty rates. African Americans are about 4.3 times more likely to be poor than whites in that cohort at ages 45 to 54, but this drops to 3.8 at ages 55 to 64 and 3.5 at ages 65 to 74. Data for Hispanics in this cohort are similar. Therefore, Cohort C seems to support the leveling hypothesis. Because official poverty rates reflect policy changes as well as demographic ones, there may be some interaction between cohort, age, and history that is confounding this picture.

As can be seen in tables 4-14 and 4-15, the pattern remains inconsistent if we look at more detailed poverty data. Table 4-15 summarizes the relationship between ethnic groups for the poorest poor (those with incomes below 75 percent of the poverty level), and the nonpoor (those with incomes twice the poverty level or more). The reader is reminded that in interpreting data for those with incomes below 75 percent of poverty, the ratio of poverty among African Americans to that of whites and that of Hispanics to whites shows leveling when it gets smaller (approaching 1.0), and indicates the jeopardy of poverty when it rises. Data for the group with incomes at twice the poverty level or higher are interpreted just the opposite. A decrease in the ratio indicates the jeopardy of poverty, while an increase (approaching 1.0) indicates leveling.

Cohort A, in going from ages 65 to 74 to ages 85 and older, generally shows a leveling effect. There is fluctuation for the poorest African Americans, but the net change for that group, and the consistent change for the other groups (best-off African Americans, and both groups of Hispanics), is toward leveling. Cohort C is more mixed, but it is also best characterized by leveling.

Although the jeopardy of poverty is mildly supported by changes in the ratio of African Americans to whites with incomes twice the poverty rate or higher, the other three ratios reflect leveling before and after the traditional retirement age. By contrast, data for Cohort B support the jeopardy of poverty. This trend is seen particularly strongly in the differences between 1970 and 1980, when this cohort moved from preretirement to postretirement ages.

The Factors That Influence Income Inequality

Chapter 3 presented a regression analysis of the sociodemographic variables that influenced family income for all three cohorts at ages 55 to 64. This chapter, which explores dynamic change within cohorts, returns to that same regression equation and estimates the parameters for three points in time.

Table 4-14. Percent Distribution of Ratio of Family Income to Poverty Level by Ethnicity,[a] Cohort, and Year

	1970			1980			1990		
Ratio	*W*	*H*	*AA*	*W*	*H*	*AA*	*W*	*H*	*AA*
COHORT A	*(Ages 65–74)*			*(Ages 75–84)*			*(Ages 85+)*		
< .75	13.2	24.4	34.5	7.1	13.0	21.6	8.8	12.7	20.7
.75–.99	7.7	12.2	13.1	8.7	14.1	17.4	9.7	14.8	19.5
1.00–1.24	7.7	8.5	10.6	11.3	9.7	13.4	11.2	10.5	13.6
1.25–1.49	7.4	8.1	7.2	9.4	9.7	9.1	8.8	11.9	8.1
1.50–1.99	12.9	11.0	10.2	14.5	17.8	13.6	13.0	10.7	12.3
2.00+	51.1	35.8	24.3	48.9	35.7	24.8	48.6	39.4	25.9
N	2,270	246	1,093	6,250	185	536	21,736	741	1,846
COHORT B	*(Ages 55–64)*			*(Ages 65–74)*			*(Ages 75–84)*		
< .75	7.3	12.9	18.4	4.5	14.11	18.6	6.3	12.5	18.3
.75–.99	3.2	5.0	8.4	5.7	8.7	13.9	7.4	15.5	18.8
1.00–1.24	3.0	4.0	7.4	6.9	12.0	11.8	8.5	10.2	12.8
1.25–1.49	3.3	5.9	6.1	6.9	10.8	8.9	8.0	8.8	9.3
1.50–1.99	7.4	12.1	12.3	13.3	17.4	13.6	13.6	13.6	12.7
2.00+	75.7	60.1	47.3	62.7	37.1	33.1	56.2	39.3	28.0
N	16,366	697	1,882	13,544	426	1,258	89,384	2,941	7,023

Table 4-14. Percent Distribution of Ratio of Family Income to Poverty Level by Ethnicity,[a] Cohort, and Year (continued)

Ratio	1970			1980			1990		
	W	*H*	*AA*	*W*	*H*	*AA*	*W*	*H*	*AA*
COHORT C	*(Ages 45–54)*			*(Ages 55–64)*			*(Ages 65–74)*		
<.75	3.9	11.9	16.9	4.3	12.9	18.4	3.9	9.4	15.6
.75–.99	1.7	4.8	6.5	2.7	5.0	8.4	4.3	9.9	13.2
1.00–1.24	2.1	8.4	6.8	2.8	4.0	7.4	5.1	8.2	10.4
1.25–1.49	2.5	7.5	6.3	3.2	5.9	6.1	5.3	6.8	8.3
1.50–1.99	6.8	10.9	12.8	6.9	12.1	12.3	10.9	12.1	12.6
2.00+	83.1	56.4	50.7	80.1	60.1	47.3	70.5	53.6	40.0
N	20,004	704	2,037	18,406	697	1,882	165,138	3,157	13,723

Source: Computed from Public Use Samples, 1960, 1970, 1980,1990

[a]For this and all tables, ethnic groups are represented by W=white, H=Hispanic, and AA=African American.

Table 4-15. Ratio of Other Ethnic Groups[a] to Whites for the Proportions with Income Less than 75 Percent of the Poverty Rate and More than 200 Percent of the Poverty Rate by Cohort and Year

	Cohort A				*Cohort B*				*Cohort C*			
	AA/W		*H/W*		*AA/W*		*H/W*		*AA/W*		*H/W*	
Year	*<.75*	*2.00+*	*<.75*	*2.00+*	*<.75*	*2.00+*	*<.75*	*2.00+*	*<.75*	*2.00+*	*<.75*	*2.00+*
1970	2.614	0.476	1.848	0.701	2.521	0.625	1.767	0.794	4.333	0.610	3.051	0.679
1980	3.042	0.507	1.831	0.730	4.133	0.528	3.133	0.592	4.279	0.591	3.000	0.750
1990	2.352	0.533	1.443	0.811	2.905	0.498	1.984	0.699	4.000	0.567	2.410	0.760

Source: Computed from table 4-14

[a]For this and all tables, ethnic groups are represented by W=white, H=Hispanic, and AA=African American.

Cohort A's Experience

Table 4-16 presents the unstandardized regression coefficients, along with the standard errors for Cohort A, at the four census dates. In addition to indicating which variables were significantly related to family income at each separate point in time, this table also presents results of a *t*-test to identify significant changes in parameters over time for the changes between 1960 and 1970 and between 1970 and 1980.

It is not possible to compute a reliable *t*-test for changes between 1980 and 1990. As explained in Chapter 2, this arose from the necessity of removing the *worked less than 48 weeks last year* variable from the 1990 equation (to eliminate multicollinearity from the high correlation between this variable and hours worked last week). Nevertheless, changes of large magnitude in estimates of variables other than occupation and hours may reasonably be assumed to be real.

Ethnicity. The most interesting negative finding is the lack of a significant influence of Hispanic ethnicity on family income when other sociodemographic differences are controlled, except in the 1990 sample in which Hispanic ethnicity predicts significantly *higher* income. Neither the insignificance of the variable in three census years nor the positive sign in the year for which it is significant (and two of the three nonsignificant estimates) eliminates the possibility of a role for overt discrimination in the generally lower incomes of Hispanics.

Such discrimination may work through discrimination in education and in a variety of occupational variables such as hiring, promotion, and layoffs. However it does suggest a less disadvantaged state for Hispanics than for African Americans, who show significant disadvantage in all four periods over and above the influences of education and occupation. Furthermore, differences among coefficient estimates across the four points in time are not significant for the variable *Hispanic.* This lack of significant differences, added to other observed patterns, suggests that the differences in Hispanic samples between 1960 and 1970 may not be extremely serious.

The effects of being African American not only influenced income significantly at all four census dates but also changed substantially over time. At ages 55 to 64, being African American subtracted $5,547 in 1990 constant dollars from family income, in addition to the effects of low education, low occupational status, living in the South and the other disadvantages of being African American represented in the list of independent variables. Consistent with the leveling hypothesis, being African American at ages 65 to 74 cost only $3,455 in constant dollars. This difference from ages 55 to 64 to ages 65 to 74 was significant at the $p < .1$ level using a two-tailed test of significance (missing the .05 level by .006).

Table 4-16. Predictors of Family Income for Cohort A

Variable	*Unstandardized b (in 1990 $)*[a]	*Standard error*[b]	t-*Statistic*[c]
	1960 (Ages 55 to 64)		
Intercept	32,476		
Hispanic	2,494	1,535.442	0.370
African American	−5,547 ***	687.865	−1.956
Female	861 *	419.555	0.411
Age	− 278 ***	60.128	−0.642
South	−3,845 ***	398.239	−0.306
Central city	1,255 **	397.946	0.394
Rural	−4,286 ***	435.020	1.835
Education	1,299 ***	49.142	1.655
Married	8,699 ***	394.434	3.680 ***
Low occupation	− 787 ***	90.858	−0.138
Hours worked	81	96.628	−5.984 ***
Worked < 48 weeks	−6,402 ***	502.331	2.644 **
	1970 (Ages 65 to 74)		
Intercept	34,812		
Hispanic	1,675	1,596.382	0.746
African American	−3,455 ***	818.835	− 6.140 ***
Female	590	510.085	0.047
Age	− 214 *	78.412	− 1.229
South	−4,037 ***	485.752	−6.587 ***
Central city	1,001 *	507.521	0.918
Rural	−5,582 ***	556.566	−12.434 ***
Education	1,169 ***	61.326	21.288 ***
Married	6,443 ***	469.071	12.686 ***
Low occupation	− 768 ***	104.213	− 7.115 ***
Hours worked	1,267 ***	173.150	6.010 ***
Worked < 48 weeks	−9,065 ***	872.976	− 7.522 ***

Table 4-16 is continued on the next page.

Table 4-16. Predictors of Family Income for Cohort A (continued)

Variable	*Unstandardized b (in 1990 $)*[a]	*Standard error*[b]
	1980 (Ages 75 to 84)	
Intercept	17,218	
Hispanic	– 8	1,564.195
African American	– 4,286 ***	958.511
Female	– 554	578.451
Age	– 68	89.146
South	– 712	532.716
Central city	– 270	613.441
Rural	– 4,790 ***	621.389
Education	707 ***	63.316
Married	2,817 ***	559.278
Low occupation	– 638 ***	167.809
Hours worked	2,030 ***	520.621
Worked < 48 weeks	– 5,241 **	1,689.719
	1990 (Ages 85+)	
Intercept	34,410	
Hispanic	3,768 ***	853.172
African American	– 2,467 ***	550.977
Female	– 1,769 ***	347.274
Age	– 95	71.474
South	– 122	305.222
Central city	– 1,182 ***	332.576
Rural	– 6,809 ***	336.204
Education	1,048 ***	41.316
Married	5,421 ***	383.630
Low occupation	– 1,594 ***	111.418
Hours worked	460 ***	39.377

Source: Computed from Public Use Samples, 1960, 1970, 1980, 1990

[a]Unstandardized regression coefficients expressed in 1990 constant dollars.

[b]Standard error before 1990 is inflated by 1.5862 to adjust constant dollars.

[c]*t*-test of the difference in estimates for the same parameter at this time and ten years later (i.e., the statistics in the 1960 portion of the table apply to the difference between 1960 and 1970 estimates).

* $p < .05$ level ** $p < .01$ level *** $p < .001$ level

Although, as discussed earlier in this chapter, the ratio of African American to white family income continued to increase as this cohort moved from ages 65 to 74 to ages 75 to 84, the separate contribution of being African American showed an increase to $4,286. While this increase is much smaller than the decrease between late middle age and young old age, it is statistically significant at the $p < .0005$ level. The influence of African American ethnicity declined again from 1980 to 1990 (to -$2,431), but this decline is not large, and may well be due to chance fluctuation.

Marital Status. A number of other variables exhibit significant changes in importance over the aging of this cohort. Being married, for example, becomes a significantly smaller economic advantage (though still a large one), from middle age in 1960 through ages 75 to 84 in 1980, probably reflecting a change from one or two paychecks to two Social Security checks. (In some cases widows or widowers move in with younger family members, in which case family income includes the income of younger family members, but this occurs in only a relatively small number of cases. See Chapter 5.)

In the ages after 85, the additional dollars associated with being married increase again to $6,443. In these ages, when the risk of nursing home placement is much higher (19.3 percent of the 1990 sample age 85 and older is living in an institution compared to 5.1 of those age 75 to 84), there is a two-way relationship between marital status and family income. First, those living with a spouse are less likely than their unmarried counterparts to be placed for similar levels of disability, and thus the family is better able to hang on to its financial resources. Second, if a married person is placed in a nursing home or other residential facility, neither spouse is counted as "married with spouse present" in the census data, and their income is no longer counted together for purposes of calculating family income.[3] Thus, those impoverished by chronic illness or mental health needs are more likely to be coded as unmarried.

Work-Related Variables. The variables related to people's work life—*usual occupation, number of hours worked last week,* and *worked less than 48 weeks last year*—change in their predictive power over the life course. It seems likely that the meaning or interpretation of these variables and the strength of their relationship with each other also changes with time. At ages 55 to 64 (1960), the effect of hours worked is not significant, but having worked less than 48 weeks in the past year costs over $6,000 and each drop in occupational status (e.g., from professional/administrative to sales, or from skilled craftsman to operative) costs almost $800.

The amount of income lost or gained with each sequential gross occupational category the person usually worked (e.g. from the unskilled–blue-collar to the skilled–blue-collar category or from clerical work to sales) remained about the same at ages 65 to 74 as it was in the working years. In many cases, respondents had the same occupational code they had at the previous census. However, once they had been retired for six years or more, they were coded as long-term unemployed for purposes of occupational categories. Working fewer than 48 weeks in the previous year cost more, and hours of work contributed more, as these variables helped differentiate the newly retired and the workers who had gone to part-time employment from those who had full and established retirement. As this cohort reached ages 75 to 84, the difference between working and not working remained important, with significant increases in the importance of hours worked (possibly reflecting the importance of part-time work in this age group), and with occupation and the number of weeks worked becoming less important. By 1990, when the group had reached ages 85 and older, so many had fully retired that the correlation between *hours worked last week* and *worked less than 48 weeks last year* was around 0.6. Thus only *hours worked* and *occupation* (correlation less than 0.5) are kept in the equation for 1990. Both variables remain significant.

Education. Each year of education completed was worth about $1,000 extra for this cohort in 1960, 1970, and 1990, but only about $700 dollars in 1980. This difference is statistically significant, but it is tempting to consider it a fluke of the sample, given its otherwise constant nature over time.

Age. The income loss associated with each additional year of life decreased slightly but not significantly as this cohort moved into late old age. *Single year of age* was statistically significant (and negative) for the two age groups in which people usually retire (55 to 64 and 65 to 74) but not significant in the later two age groups.

Gender. Being a woman was a significant economic advantage (with other factors controlled) in the preretirement ages and a significant economic disadvantage in the oldest age, with values in the intervening years that are not significant but mark a consistent direction of change. The disadvantage of women in the oldest years, with all of these variables controlled, may be related to their greater likelihood of impairment and impoverishment through chronic care expenses. The advantage in the earlier ages will reflect a difference between unmarried men and women in these ages. The women will be disproportionately widows, many collecting some kind of benefits from their late husbands. The men are much more likely to be never-married men—a group known to have relatively low earning power.

Place of Residence. The other three variables may reflect historical rather than cohort changes. They are the residential variables: *southern residence*, *rural residence*, and *central-city residence*. The economic disadvantages of rural and southern residence were both statistically significant in 1960 and 1970, and they did not change significantly between these two dates. The effects of rurality remained negative and statistically significant during the next two decades, but decreased significantly from 1970 to 1980, and increased again, by a fairly substantial margin, from 1980 to 1990. At these same two points, the effect of rural residence became so small that it was not significant, though it remained negative. Central-city residence showed a statistically significant positive influence on income in 1960 and 1970, was not significant in 1980, and had a significant *negative* influence in 1990. Whether these changes in the importance and direction of place of residence variables reflect a period or cohort change will be demonstrated, in part, by comparing changes in the other two cohorts for the same time period. However, this will not take into consideration interactions between age and period that would occur, for example if benefits for retirement became more equitable across regions or size of place but wages and salaries did not.

Cohort B's Experience

Ethnicity. In Cohort B, as in Cohort A, the independent influence of Hispanic ethnicity was not significant in 1960, 1970, and 1980, and was significant in the positive direction in 1990. The influence of African American ethnicity was significant at each age, but grew significantly smaller with each increase in age, until stabilizing at around $3,000 for the two postretirement age groups in 1980 and 1990 (see table 4-17), thus supporting the leveling hypothesis. This pattern mirrors that of Cohort A, in that it shows a significant decline in the influence of African American ethnicity on income from the immediate preretirement to the immediate postretirement years. However, it is somewhat different from Cohort A in showing the same influence across the postretirement years, while Cohort A showed some fluctuation during that period. On the other hand, the two cohorts are alike in showing the same influence in 1980 and 1990, suggesting an historical rather than a cohort effect producing this stabilization. Nevertheless, to the extent that any age difference in the influence of ethnicity is demonstrated, it supports the leveling hypothesis.

For the two preretirement age groups in this cohort, the negative effect of being African American decreased significantly from 1960 to 1970. This shows an historical change that did not come entirely through changes in the occupational variables such as reductions in layoffs or large occupational changes, since these are controlled in this equation. It is possible that the improvement did occur because of reductions in other types of workplace discrimination (potential examples are equal pay for equal work or chances for small advancements, which do not show up in the very broad occupational categories necessitated by these data).

Marital Status. During the years before retirement (1960 and 1970), when incomes were rising and women were returning to the work force, the financial advantage of being married also increased from about $11,000 in 1990 dollars to over $13,600. However, as the cohort reached retirement age, the marital advantage decreased significantly, just as it had for Cohort A. Unlike the experience of Cohort A, and like their own experience with ethnicity, members of Cohort B did not see a continuing decline from ages 65 to 74 to ages 75 to 84, but rather a stabilization.

Work-Related Variables. There are more changes in the predictive power of these variables within the preretirement years for Cohort B than might be expected. The effects of layoffs, job changes, and other interruptions, shown in *working less than 48 weeks in the past year*, remain about the same. However, *number of hours worked* goes from a nonsignificant contribution in 1960 (ages 45 to 54) to a significant one (about $400 in annual constant-dollar income for each additional hour per week of work) in 1970. This suggests that the rise of part-time work may occur before the conventional retirement ages in this group. *Low occupational status* also has a higher cost at ages 55 to 64 than it had for ages 45 to 54 in this cohort.

The occupational and work force variables only somewhat parallel the age-related changes demonstrated in Cohort A in the three age groups they have in common. As in Cohort A, the number of hours per week worked are worth significantly more after age 65 than before. Working fewer than 48 weeks appears to show greater liability at age

65 to 74 than at age 55 to 64, as was also seen in Cohort A, though in Cohort B the difference is not statistically significant. By contrast, low occupational status becomes less important after retirement (until 1990 with its altered equation), while for Cohort A it remained stable until this point.

Table 4-17. Predictors of Family Income for Cohort B

Variable	*Unstandardized b (in 1990 $)*[a]	*Standard error*[b]	t-*Statistic*[c]
	1960 (Ages 45 to 54)		
Intercept	6,113		
Hispanic	– 2,011	1,287.030	–1.144
African American	– 7,576 ***	562.963	–3.122 **
Female	1,255 ***	359.983	1.807 *
Age	67	50.448	7.266 ***
South	– 3,978 ***	332.756	1.460
Central city	1,296 ***	346.137	1.852 *
Rural	– 4,506 ***	364.929	4.221 ***
Education	1,780 ***	46.687	–3.367 ***
Married	11,175 ***	393.290	–4.171 ***
Low occupation	– 592 ***	79.940	2.961 **
Hours worked	– 59	81.047	–3.462 ***
Worked < 48 weeks	– 5,553 ***	406.437	0.336
	1970 (Ages 55 to 64)		
Intercept	42,383		
Hispanic	76	1,293.606	– 0.387
African American	– 4,752 ***	707.872	– 2.081 *
Female	230	438.129	0.673
Age	– 539 ***	66.403	– 5.804 ***
South	– 4,760 ***	419.716	– 7.950 ***
Central city	260	439.227	0.244
Rural	– 7,074 ***	486.822	– 5.523 ***
Education	2,032 ***	58.582	11.336 ***
Married	13,637 ***	440.134	9.442 ***
Low occupation	– 966 ***	97.648	– 1.825 *
Hours worked	401 ***	105.149	– 4.833 ***
Worked < 48 weeks	– 5,782 ***	544.692	– 0.955

Table 4-17 is continued on the next page

Table 4-17. Predictors of Family Income for Cohort B (continued)

Variable	*Unstandardized b (in 1990 $)*[a]	*Standard error*[b]
	1980 (Ages 65 to 74)	
Intercept	17,018	
Hispanic	703	973.492
African American	– 2,825 ***	597.274
Female	– 146	346.175
Age	– 33	56.486
South	– 476	337.975
Central city	406	405.791
Rural	– 3,626 ***	390.822
Education	1,199 ***	44.331
Married	8,353 ***	345.589
Low occupation	– 742 ***	73.514
Hours worked	1,428 ***	184.600
Worked < 48 weeks	– 6,616 ***	683.457
	1990 (Ages 75 to 84)	
Intercept	21,630	
Hispanic	3,088 ***	453.704
African American	– 2,799 ***	302.194
Female	– 694 ***	173.035
Age	– 48	27.249
South	– 597 ***	163.816
Central city	– 366 *	182.906
Rural	– 6,908 ***	183.089
Education	1,677 ***	23.874
Married	8,702 ***	168.502
Low occupation	– 1,406 ***	46.406
Hours worked	382 ***	12.433

Source: Computed from Public Use Samples, 1960, 1970, 1980, 1990

[a]Unstandardized regression coefficients expressed in 1990 constant dollars.

[b]Standard error before 1990 is inflated by 1.5862 to adjust constant dollars.

[c]*t*-test of the difference in estimates for the same parameter at this time and ten years later (i.e., the statistics in the 1960 portion of the table apply to the difference between 1960 and 1970 estimates).

* $p < .05$ level   ** $p < .01$ level   *** $p < .001$ level

Education. This cohort, with two preretirement age groups, demonstrates what may be an historical increase in the financial importance of education for working people from 1960 to 1970 (ages 45 to 54 to ages 55 to 64), and a significant decline in the importance of education in the immediate postretirement years. This shows a substantial rise again in the 75 to 84 age group, but still remains less important than in the preretirement years. (Both Cohorts A and B show the smallest advantage of education in 1980, but it is difficult to imagine what historical factors or sample oddities might account for this finding, and it does not hold for Cohort C.)

Age. In the age span 55 to 64, each single year of age was significantly associated with income loss. This finding parallels the experience of Cohort A. Unlike Cohort A, where this variable was also significant for the immediate postretirement age, it is not significant for any other age span in Cohort B.

Gender. As in Cohort A, gender is significant only for 1960 and 1990, though these years represent different ages for the two cohorts. The two cohorts are parallel in showing gender as a positive predictor of family income when significant in a preretirement age, and a negative predictor when significant postretirement.

Place of Residence. The effects of living in the South and in rural areas were increasingly negative in the working years from 1960 to 1970, but of declining significance in the immediate postretirement ages as measured in 1980. However, in 1990 the effect of the two variables were quite different. *Southern residence* showed about the same negative effect that it had in 1980, while that of *rural residence* more than doubled.

Central-city residence shows the same pattern it did in Cohort A, significantly positive in 1960, not significant in 1970 and 1980, and significantly negative for 1990. This, again, appears to reflect historical rather than life-course changes in the influence of place of residence.

Cohort C's Experience

Ethnicity. Hispanic ethnicity is positively related to family income in 1990 for this cohort, as for all of the others. Since it is positive for five of the six age-cohort combinations over the age of 65, and significant for the three (all in 1990) with large sample sizes, this strongly suggests a true positive effect for older Hispanics when other demographic characteristics are controlled. The effect of Hispanic ethnicity on younger adults is less clear. It is significantly negative for the Cohort C at the youngest age examined (age 35 to 44 in 1960), but it is not significant and of varying sign for the remaining younger ages.

As in the other two cohorts, African American ethnicity has a significant effect on income at each age for Cohort C. There is not a significant difference in the ethnic effect from ages 35 to 44 to ages 45 to 54, but there are significant declines for the remaining ages. This stability in the younger ages suggests that the leveling demonstrated in the older cohorts was, indeed, leveling with age and not a universal, historical reduction in income inequality.

Marital Status. The financial advantages of being married in Cohort C roughly paralleled those in Cohort B. It increases significantly from 1960 to 1970 and then begins to decline in significance. It differs from Cohort B in that it shows a decline in the importance of this variable from ages 45 to 54 to ages 55 to 64, while there was an increase at this point in Cohort B. This is likely due to historical factors increasing family income between 1960 and 1970.

Work-Related Variables. Cohort C's experience confirms the finding for Cohort B that part time work becomes important in the 55 to 64 age group, leading to a significant contribution of hours worked at that age and in the postretirement age, but not at the younger ages. They are also alike in that working fewer than 48 weeks has a similar effect at ages 45 to 54 and 55 to 64. In Cohort C layoffs and other interruptions also have a greater negative effect on constant-dollar income at the older preretirement ages (45 to 54 and 55 to 64) than at the younger time.

Education. Education is a significant predictor of income at every age for Cohort C, as it is for the other cohorts. However, the fluctuations among ages do not show any distinct pattern or parallel to other cohorts.

Age. Cohort C, like the other cohorts, saw a significant decrease in income with each additional year in the age group 55 to 64. It saw an even larger decrease for each year in the age group 45 to 54—a finding not consistent with Cohort B's experience.

Gender. In Cohort C, gender was positive and significant for the two youngest ages. It is parallel to the experience of other cohorts in that all cohorts found that when gender is significant before retirement ages it is positive. Gender was not a significant predictor in the postretirement age for this cohort. (In other cohorts it was negative whenever it was significant in these age groups.)

Table 4-18. Predictors of Family Income for Cohort C

Variable	*Unstandardized b (in 1990 $)*[a]	*Standard error*[b]	t-*Statistic*[c]
	1960 (Ages 35 to 44)		
Intercept	–9,275		
Hispanic	–1,602 *	673.210	– 1.391
African American	–7,062 ***	323.023	– 1.617
Female	3,001 ***	222.538	1.634
Age	427 ***	29.949	9.606 ***
South	–2,727 ***	194.833	1.154
Central city	– 297	206.926	– 0.234
Rural	–4,781 ***	218.306	2.548 **
Education	1,767 ***	29.814	–11.484 ***
Married	8,968 ***	250.956	–15.245 ***
Low occupation	– 595 ***	46.049	5.669 ***
Hours worked	78	48.174	0.882
Worked < 48 weeks	–4,243 ***	244.679	2.609 **
	1970 (Ages 45 to 54)		
Intercept	16,847		
Hispanic	113	1,032.630	0.613
African American	– 5,893 ***	646.541	–1.678 *
Female	2,238 ***	410.101	3.283 **
Age	– 220 ***	60.350	4.328 ***
South	– 3,226 ***	386.827	–2.951 ***
Central city	– 189	411.417	–1.635
Rural	– 6,066 ***	454.811	–1.515
Education	2,527 ***	58.989	9.150 ***
Married	16,818 ***	449.624	1.859 *
Low occupation	– 1,188 ***	93.965	–1.914 *
Hours worked	– 17	96.506	–4.595 ***
Worked < 48 weeks	– 5,677 ***	492.228	.121

Table 4-18 is continued on the next page.

Table 4-18. Predictors of Family Income for Cohort C (continued)

Variable	*Unstandardized b (in 1990 $)*[a]	*Standard error*[b]	t-*Statistic*[c]
	1980 (Ages 55 to 64)		
Intercept	41,904		
Hispanic	– 720	883.689	
African American	– 4,440 ***	576.200	
Female	493	338.308	
Age	– 573 ***	54.575	
South	– 1,716 ***	335.029	
Central city	747	398.193	
Rural	– 5,150 ***	402.754	
Education	1,821 ***	49.710	
Married	15,735 ***	370.892	
Low occupation	– 955 ***	77.085	
Hours worked	674 ***	115.499	
Worked < 48 weeks	– 6,435 ***	464.187	
	1990 (Ages 65 to 74)		
Intercept	6,346		
Hispanic	965 *	487.803	
African American	– 2,722 ***	247.773	
Female	– 8	135.645	
Age	31	22.919	
South	– 653 ***	138.347	
Central city	– 117	153.290	
Rural	– 7,609 ***	155.896	
Education	2,308 ***	22.257	
Married	12,922 ***	140.172	
Low occupation	– 1,191 ***	29.456	
Hours worked	353 ***	5.732	

Source: Computed from Public Use Samples, 1960, 1970, 1980, 1990
[a]Unstandardized regression coefficients expressed in 1990 constant dollars.
[b]Standard error before 1990 is inflated by 1.5862 to adjust constant dollars.
[c]*t*-test of the difference in estimates for the same parameter at this time and ten years later (i.e., the statistics in the 1960 portion of the table apply to the difference between 1960 and 1970 estimates).
* $p < .05$ level ** $p < .01$ level *** $p < .001$ level

Place of Residence. These variables show a clear-cut pattern for Cohort C, though not entirely consistent with the experiences of the other two cohorts. Central-city residence is not significant for this cohort at any time-age interval. Living in the South is a financial liability, but its "cost" decreases from the younger ages to preretirement and from pre- to postretirement. The liability associated with rural residence, by contrast, becomes increasingly strong over the four decades. The patterns are less consistent in other cohorts, but they also show a general weakening of the *southern residence* variable and strengthening of the *rural* one. This trend appears to be at least partly historical in that there is more consistency among time periods than age groups when comparing the three groups, however interactions with the cohort life cycle may account for some of the fluctuations observed.

The Factors That Influence Poverty

Because ethnic differences in the likelihood of poverty are not as consistent in their support of the leveling hypothesis as are differences in family income, separate equations were estimated with the same dependent variables but using the ratio of the family's income to poverty as the independent variable. By the nature of this variable, the larger (more positive) the parameter, the smaller the likelihood of poverty. For example, in table 4-19 the positive value of being female at ages 55 to 64 and the significantly different negative value of that variable at ages 65 to 74 means that being a woman in the immediate postretirement years decreases the chances of poverty, but increases the odds of poverty for the two later age groups. The unstandardized coefficients themselves may be interpreted as percentage points. Thus, continuing to use gender as an example, if a man of some given combination of characteristics representing the other variables in the equation had an income at the poverty line (ratio =1.000), a woman with the same combination of characteristics would expect an income just above the poverty line (ratio = 1.000 + 0.148 = 1.148).

Cohort A's Experience

Because of the absence of poverty data in 1960, the jeopardy of poverty hypothesis cannot be examined in the data for Cohort A. However, it is worth noting some differences in the postretirement experience of Cohort A when we focus on the likelihood of poverty rather than overall family income. The most important of these is that Hispanic ethnicity is a significant predictor of poverty in both 1970 and 1980 (ages 65 to 74 and 75 to 84), though it was not significantly related to overall income differences in those age-year groups. In 1990, when the influence of Hispanic ethnicity on family income was significantly *positive*, that status no longer shows a significant relationship to poverty. Since relationship to poverty is a factor of both total family income and total family size, this overall pattern suggests that the extended family structure of some older Hispanics may be contributing to a relatively large family income, but that this income must meet the needs of a larger group of people.

African American ethnicity is a significant predictor of poverty at all three periods, but somewhat less strongly for the oldest age group. This provides slight support to the idea of leveling across the life course.

Cohort B's Experience

The mechanism for the jeopardy of poverty hypothesis can be tested in Cohort B, for which there are data at one preretirement age and two postretirement. ages table 4-20 shows that while both ethnic statuses are significantly related to poverty status at all three points in time, there was no significant change in the effects of ethnicity for the years for which a reliable *t*-test can be constructed. Since this period represents the change from preretirement to postretirement, it suggests no change in the effect of ethnicity on poverty over time when other variables are controlled, thus supporting neither the leveling nor the jeopardy of poverty hypothesis.

It was shown earlier in the chapter that African American and Hispanic elders in this cohort do experience greater increases in poverty than whites. However, these regression findings suggest that this change probably occurs through changes in other statuses related to poverty. Some of these are captured in the equation, such as greater marital disruption. Some others (such as qualifying for Social Security benefits) will be discussed in Chapter 5.

Cohort C's Experience

Poverty data are available for Cohort C at two preretirement ages and one postretirement age. These data show a somewhat different picture for Hispanics and African Americans. These two groups are alike in that ethnicity is a significant predictor of poverty at all three time points for both, showing that both Hispanics and African Americans are more likely to be poor than whites even when marital status, work-related variables and place-of-residence variables are controlled. There are some changes in the magnitude of the coefficients for ethnic status in Cohort C in contrast to the stability of these coefficients in Cohort B.

Table 4-19. Factors That Predict Ratio of Family Income to the Poverty Level for Cohort A

Variable	b^a	*Standard error*	t-*Statistic*^{b}
	1970 (65 to 74)		
Intercept	6.396		
Hispanic	−0.274 *	0.115	0.401
African American	−0.727 ***	0.059	0.477
Female	0.148 ***	0.037	4.397 ***
Age	−0.030 ***	0.006	−1.988 *
South	−0.461 ***	0.035	−2.855 **
Central city	−0.103 **	0.037	0.764
Rural	−0.330 ***	0.040	2.615 **
Education	0.075 ***	0.004	0.702
Married	0.796 ***	0.034	3.784 ***
Low occupation	−0.096 ***	0.008	−3.916 ***
Hours worked	0.078 ***	0.012	0.089
Worked < 48 weeks	−0.625 ***	0.063	−0.760
	1980 (75 to 84)		
Intercept	5.516		
Hispanic	−0.342 *	0.124	
African American	−0.773 ***	0.076	
Female	−0.111 *	0.046	
Age	−0.012	0.007	
South	−0.304 ***	0.042	
Central city	0.056	0.049	
Rural	−0.497 ***	0.049	
Education	0.070 ***	0.005	
Married	0.585 ***	0.045	
Low occupation	−0.036 *	0.013	
Hours worked	0.074	0.041	
Worked < 48 weeks	−0.512 ***	0.134	

Table 4-19. Factors That Predict Ratio of Family Income to the Poverty Level for Cohort A (continued)

Variable	b^a	*Standard error*	t-*Statistic*[b]
	1990 (Ages 85+)		
Intercept	6.682		
Hispanic	0.005	0.056	
African American	–0.320 ***	0.036	
Female	–0.149 ***	0.023	
Age	–0.049 ***	0.005	
South	–0.044 *	0.020	
Central city	–0.008	0.022	
Rural	–0.379 ***	0.022	
Education	0.074 ***	0.003	
Married	0.552 ***	0.025	
Low occupation	–0.127 ***	0.007	
Hours worked	0.018 ***	0.003	

Source: Computed from Public Use Samples, 1960, 1970, 1980, 1990
[a]Unstandardized regression coefficients
[b]*t*-test of the difference in estimates for the same parameter at this time and ten years later (i.e., the statistics in the 1960 portion of the table apply to the difference between 1960 and 1970 estimates).
* $p < .05$ level ** $p < .01$ level *** $p < .001$ level

Hispanic ethnicity predicts a significantly smaller change in poverty for the immediate preretirement age group than for the younger age (45 to 54). Then the effect appears to level off with the immediate postretirement group in 1990. This gives mild additional support to the leveling demonstrated in the actual poverty rates of Hispanics earlier in this chapter.

African American ethnicity also seems to support leveling, but on a different time schedule. For that group, the influence of ethnicity on poverty is about the same at both younger ages and drops at the postretirement age. Because this change takes place between 1980 and 1990, for which times the equations are necessarily slightly different, a direct test of this difference is not valid. However, the size of the difference is such that it would be significant if the equations were perfectly matched, and the similarity of the Hispanic estimates for the same period *suggests* that the difference is not due to this difference in the equations.

Table 4-20. Factors That Predict Ratio of Family Income to the Poverty Level for Cohort B

Variable	b^a	*Standard error*	t-*Statistic*[b]
	1970 (Age 55 to 64)		
Intercept	5.449		
Hispanic	−0.506 ***	0.071	−1.195
African American	−0.701 ***	0.039	1.095
Female	0.250 ***	0.024	6.651 ***
Age	−0.020 ***	0.004	−1.370
South	−0.430 ***	0.023	−4.798 ***
Central city	0.099 ***	0.024	2.075 *
Rural	−0.240 ***	0.027	1.395
Education	0.062 ***	0.003	−3.696 ***
Married	0.864 ***	0.024	1.590
Low occupation	−0.051 ***	0.005	0.513
Hours worked	0.066 ***	0.006	2.858 **
Worked < 48 weeks	−0.600 ***	0.030	−2.891 **
	1980 (Age 65 to 74)		
Intercept	5.257		
Hispanic	−0.385 ***	0.072	
African American	−0.766 ***	0.044	
Female	0.016	0.026	
Age	−0.012 **	0.004	
South	−0.267 ***	0.025	
Central city	0.019	0.030	
Rural	−0.295 ***	0.029	
Education	0.079 ***	0.003	
Married	0.808 ***	0.026	
Low occupation	−0.055 ***	0.006	
Hours worked	0.024	0.014	
Worked < 48 weeks	−0.430 ***	0.051	

Table 4-20 is continued on the next page.

Table 4-20. Factors That Predict Ratio of Family Income to the Poverty Level for Cohort B (continued)

Variable	b^a		*Standard error*	t-*Statistic*[b]
	1990 (Age 75 to 84)			
Intercept	3.623			
Hispanic	–0.160	***	0.026	
African American	–0.475	***	0.018	
Female	–0.093	***	0.010	
Age	–0.022	***	0.002	
South	–0.097	***	0.010	
Central city	–0.011		0.011	
Rural	–0.441	***	0.011	
Education	0.132	***	0.001	
Married	0.656	***	0.010	
Low occupation	–0.084	***	0.003	
Hours worked	0.013	***	0.001	

Source: Computed from Public Use Samples, 1960, 1970, 1980, 1990

[a]Unstandardized regression coefficients

[b]*t*-test of the difference in estimates for the same parameter at this time and ten years later (i.e., the statistics in the 1960 portion of the table apply to the difference between 1960 and 1970 estimates).

* $p < .05$ level ** $p < .01$ level *** $p < .001$ level

Summary

The cohort analysis in this chapter has strongly supported the leveling hypothesis, which states that ethnic differences in income will become smaller as a cohort ages beyond the usual retirement years. Generally narrowing differences in median family income and family income quartiles among African Americans, Hispanics, and whites are seen in all three cohorts as they move from middle age to early old age, though the changes are not unilateral in all cases. This difference occurs primarily because of the proportionately smaller income declines that accompany aging for the two minority groups. Regression analysis reveals that the direct effects of African American ethnicity, but not Hispanic ethnicity, on income are significant both before and into old age, but, with minor fluctuations, these effects decline in later years consistent with the leveling hypothesis.

Table 4-21. Factors That Predict Ratio of Family Income to the Poverty Level for Cohort C

Variable	*b*[a]	*Standard error*	t-*Statistic*[b]
	1970 (Age 45 to 54)		
Intercept	3.942		
Hispanic	−0.460 ***	0.046	−2.554 **
African American	−0.684 ***	0.029	0.366
Female	0.304 ***	0.018	5.267 ***
Age	0.005	0.003	0.729
South	−0.252 ***	0.017	−1.827 *
Central city	0.113 ***	0.018	4.145 ***
Rural	−0.155 ***	0.020	0.953
Education	0.068 ***	0.003	3.453 ***
Married	0.687 ***	0.020	−5.559 ***
Low occupation	−0.023 ***	0.004	3.623 ***
Hours worked	0.042 ***	0.004	1.079
Worked < 48 weeks	−0.530 ***	0.022	0.727
	1980 (Age 55 to 64)		
Intercept	4.426		
Hispanic	−0.285 ***	0.051	
African American	−0.700 ***	0.033	
Female	0.164 ***	0.019	
Age	0.002	0.003	
South	−0.205 ***	0.019	
Central city	−0.008	0.023	
Rural	−0.184 ***	0.023	
Education	0.055 ***	0.003	
Married	0.849 ***	0.021	
Low occupation	−0.045 ***	0.004	
Hours worked	0.034 ***	0.007	
Worked < 48 weeks	−0.555 ***	0.026	

Table 4-21 is continued on the next page.

Table 4-21. Factors That Predict Ratio of Family Income to the Poverty Level for Cohort C (continued)

Variable	b^a	*Standard error*	t-*Statistic*^{b}
	1990 (Age 65 to 74)		
Intercept	1.928		
Hispanic	–0.326 ***	0.023	
African American	–0.541 ***	0.012	
Female	–0.017 *	0.007	
Age	–0.005 ***	0.001	
South	–0.078 ***	0.007	
Central city	0.006	0.007	
Rural	–0.446 ***	0.008	
Education	0.153 ***	0.001	
Married	0.809 ***	0.007	
Low occupation	–0.073 ***	0.001	
Hours worked	0.012 ***	0.000	

Source: Computed from Public Use Samples, 1960, 1970, 1980, 1990
[a]Unstandardized regression coefficients
[b]*t*-test of the difference in estimates for the same parameter at this time and ten years later (i.e., the statistics in the 1960 portion of the table apply to the difference between 1960 and 1970 estimates).
* $p < .05$ level   ** $p < .01$ level   *** $p < .001$ level

Each successively younger cohort has higher constant-dollar income than the one preceding it, but the constant-dollar income inequality within cohorts shows little or no improvement when cohorts are compared at the same ages. The one exception is an increase of income for Hispanics in all age groups for 1990, which may be an artifact of the larger sample.

Cohort C, unlike Cohort B, showed income decline between ages 45 to 54 and 55 to 64 and an accompanying increase in ethnic inequality between those two age-time points. These appear to be related to the more difficult economic climate in 1980. (Only Cohort C was still in middle age in that year.) Factors that influenced income declines compared to income increases in Cohort B between the same two age categories were: (1) greater changes in the proportion employed for the whole year in Cohort C; greater losses in real income for those who were not employed for the whole year in Cohort C; and declining real income for the fully employed in Cohort C, compared to increasing real income for the fully employed in Cohort B.

Although data support the leveling of overall income for all cohorts, the cohorts differ in the relationship they experience between ethnicity and poverty. In Cohort B, both Hispanics and African Americans show higher percentages in poverty relative to whites in the postretirement ages than in the preretirement ages, supporting the jeopardy of poverty hypothesis. The opposite is true of Cohort C. Although African Americans and Hispanics are still more likely to be poor, the poverty of these groups relative to whites declines with each successive decade.

Though there was no significant effect of Hispanic ethnic status on overall income distribution except for a significant *positive* effect in 1990, there was a significant direct effect on the likelihood of poverty at all points in time for all cohorts, suggesting a difference in family structure between Hispanics and the other two ethnic groups.

Notes

[1]The gains by African Americans are small and may reflect small differences in the sample, though it is also seen in Cohort B for the same time period. The somewhat larger gains of Hispanics may be an artifact of the much larger sample size in 1990 than in the previous years. It does not appear to be related to the problem of including some members of the older cohort (see Chapter 2), because the same phenomenon is seen for Cohort B between 1980 and 1990 (see below). It is also possible that changes in income supports or selective mortality may have a stronger overall effect on these two poorer populations, such that their constant-dollar income really *did* increase from 1980 to 1990.

[2]If the person placed in a nursing home receives funding through Medicaid (as most do if their stay exceeds six months), he or she will be allowed to keep only a small allowance for toilet articles and such minor personal expenses, with the rest going to Medicaid to help defray costs.

[3]Poverty is calculated only for those not living in institutions.

V
Family, Other Resources, and Government Assistance

The two preceding analytical chapters have dealt with family income as a measure of financial well-being. Such a measure is incomplete for any age group. For the aged, most of whose resources do not come *directly* from employment income, family income may be a particularly incomplete subset of resources. While there have been a number of efforts to incorporate measures of income with measures of wealth, none of them is entirely successful, and none of those which attempt to produce a single composite score is applicable to census data (O'Rand, 1982).[1]

This chapter begins by examining ethnic, gender, and cohort differences in living arrangements that are simultaneously sources, expressions, and results of financial as well as social well-being. It then examines ethnic differences in assets—home ownership, savings, and investments. Finally it looks at the role of government transfers. How do living arrangement, assets, and government contribute to double jeopardy or leveling? How are they changing through successive cohorts?

Living Arrangements

Preferences

There is a hierarchy of living arrangement preferences in the United States that cuts across age and income lines, though not necessarily ethnic boundaries. People prefer to live independently (with a spouse if married, or alone if not). Living with other family members is less desirable than independence; but much more desirable than institutionalization (Staples and Mirande, 1980; Troll, 1971).

One's ability to live in the more desirable arrangement is determined by a complex interplay of cultural, social, economic, demographic, and health variables. Some of these can be measured directly using census data and some indirectly; some cannot be measured with these data; and a few may be immeasurable. Therefore, examining ethnic and life-course differences in living arrangements using census data can only suggest some part of the explanation. Because there are traditional sex-role norms as well as other sources of gender differences in living arrangements, men and women in each cohort will be discussed separately.

Living as Head or Spouse

Table 5-1 shows that in all three cohorts and at all four points in time, most people had the preferred living arrangement—as the head of household or the spouse of the head.[2] It is also true that white men and women were more likely to be living in this arrangement than African American or Hispanic people of the same gender and age group for each point. There are, however, some differences among ethnic groups, between the sexes, and over time within the sex/ethnic groups.

Table 5-1. Percent in Selected Relationships to Head of Household by Sex, Ethnicity,[a] Cohort, and Census Year

	Men (Percent)			*Women (Percent)*		
Relationship	*W*	*H*	*AA*	*W*	*H*	*AA*
COHORT A, 1960 (Ages 55 to 64)						
Relatives						
Head/spouse	91.1	89.3	84.7	86.5	80.2	78.0
Child[b]	1.0	0.0	1.7	1.3	0.0	2.5
Parent[c]	1.2	3.6	1.9	4.5	9.3	7.8
Sibling[d]	2.1	0.9	2.1	2.1	3.5	2.0
Other	0.6	1.8	1.5	1.8	5.8	2.3
Subtotal	95.9	95.5	91.9	96.1	98.8	92.5
Nonrelatives						
Roomer/boarder	1.5	0.0	6.0	0.9	1.2	3.1
Patient/resident[e]	1.6	1.8	1.0	1.3	0.0	1.9
Other	1.0	2.7	1.0	1.7	0.0	2.5
Subtotal	4.1	4.5	8.1	3.9	1.2	7.5
N	6,760	112	581	7,301	86	644

Table 5-1 is continued on the next page.

Table 5-1. Percent in Selected Relationships to Head of Household by Sex, Ethnicity,[a] Cohort, and Census Year (continued)

	Men (Percent)			*Women (Percent)*		
Relationship	*W*	*H*	*AA*	*W*	*H*	*AA*
COHORT A, 1970 (Ages 65 to 74)						
Relatives						
Head/spouse	91.7	79.7	84.5	84.7	70.0	79.3
Child[b]	0.4	0.0	1.0	0.5	0.8	1.1
Parent[c]	1.8	10.6	3.6	7.3	20.0	8.6
Sibling[d]	1.9	1.6	2.0	2.4	1.5	3.6
Other	0.3	0.8	1.4	1.3	3.1	2.1
Subtotal	96.1	92.7	92.4	96.3	95.4	94.8
Nonrelatives						
Roomer/boarder	1.3	0.8	4.0	0.6	1.5	2.1
Patient/resident[e]	2.1	3.3	2.8	1.8	1.5	1.6
Other	0.5	3.3	0.8	1.3	1.5	1.5
Subtotal	3.9	7.4	7.6	3.7	4.5	5.2
N	4,876	123	503	6,220	130	614
COHORT A, 1980 (Ages 75 to 84)						
Relatives						
Head/spouse	88.0	78.5	79.0	75.3	61.9	72.2
Child[b]	0.0	0.0	0.0	0.1	1.0	0.5
Parent[c]	4.1	10.8	4.9	10.9	28.9	14.0
Sibling[d]	0.8	4.3	2.0	2.4	2.1	3.2
Other	0.6	0.0	1.5	0.7	1.0	1.3
Subtotal	93.5	93.5	87.3	89.3	94.8	91.3
Nonrelatives						
Roomer/boarder	0.5	0.0	0.0	0.4	3.1	1.9
Patient/resident[e]	5.6	4.3	11.7	9.7	2.1	6.1
Other	0.4	2.2	1.0	0.6	0.0	0.8
Subtotal	6.5	6.5	12.7	10.7	5.2	8.7
N	2,417	93	205	4,361	97	378

Table 5-1 is continued on the next page.

Table 5-1. Percent in Selected Relationships to Head of Household by Sex, Ethnicity,[a] Cohort, and Census Year (continued)

	Men (Percent)			*Women (Percent)*		
Relationship	*W*	*H*	*AA*	*W*	*H*	*AA*
COHORT A, 1990 (Ages 85+)						
Relatives						
Head/spouse	76.4	65.4	71.4	60.1	43.3	57.6
Child[b]	0.0	0.0	0.0	0.0	0.0	0.0
Parent[c]	5.0	13.1	9.5	8.9	26.0	14.6
Sibling[d]	0.6	1.2	1.7	1.3	1.6	2.3
Other	2.5	8.1	4.3	5.0	14.2	8.3
Subtotal	84.5	87.8	86.9	75.3	85.1	82.7
Nonrelatives						
Roomer/boarder	0.6	0.3	1.1	0.6	1.8	0.8
Patient/resident[e]	14.0	9.7	10.1	23.3	11.0	15.2
Other	0.8	2.2	2.0	0.7	2.2	1.3
Subtotal	15.4	12.2	13.2	24.7	15.0	17.3
N	7,651	321	654	19,596	501	1,475
COHORT B, 1960 (Ages 45 to 54)						
Relatives						
Head/spouse	92.0	87.5	82.4	91.2	87.9	83.6
Child[b]	2.8	1.4	2.6	3.3	6.1	2.5
Parent[c]	0.2	1.4	0.3	1.0	2.3	3.4
Sibling[d]	1.5	2.8	2.7	1.7	0.8	3.5
Other	0.3	1.4	2.2	0.2	0.8	1.5
Subtotal	96.8	94.5	90.2	97.4	97.9	94.5
Nonrelatives						
Roomer/boarder	0.9	2.8	6.5	0.8	0.0	2.8
Patient/resident[e]	1.4	1.4	2.2	0.9	0.0	1.3
Other	0.8	1.4	1.0	1.0	2.3	1.5
Subtotal	3.1	5.6	9.7	2.7	2.3	5.6
N	9,074	144	876	9,322	132	953

Table 5-1 is continued on the next page.

Table 5-1. Percent in Selected Relationships to Head of Household by Sex, Ethnicity,[a] Cohort, and Census Year (continued)

	Men (Percent)			*Women (Percent)*		
Relationship	*W*	*H*	*AA*	*W*	*H*	*AA*
COHORT B, 1970 (Ages 55 to 64)						
Relatives						
Head/spouse	94.0	90.5	85.3	90.7	83.6	84.5
Child[b]	1.0	0.9	1.9	1.3	0.5	2.2
Parent[c]	0.5	0.9	1.2	2.8	12.6	5.6
Sibling[d]	1.5	1.9	2.1	2.2	1.4	2.4
Other	0.1	1.4	1.0	0.2	0.5	1.2
Subtotal	97.1	95.6	91.5	97.2	98.6	95.9
Nonrelatives						
Roomer/boarder	0.7	1.4	4.2	0.6	0.5	1.2
Patient/resident[e]	1.5	1.4	2.3	0.9	0.0	0.9
Other	0.7	1.4	1.9	1.2	0.9	2.1
Subtotal	2.9	4.2	8.4	2.7	1.4	4.2
N	7,784	211	771	8,782	214	863
COHORT B, 1980 (Ages 65 to 74)						
Relatives						
Head/spouse	93.8	87.1	88.8	89.8	75.2	83.5
Child[b]	0.2	0.5	0.2	0.3	1.7	0.0
Parent[c]	1.5	4.1	2.2	3.8	15.5	6.5
Sibling[d]	1.2	1.5	1.7	2.3	2.1	3.8
Other	0.3	1.5	1.3	0.5	2.1	1.7
Subtotal	97.0	94.7	94.2	96.7	96.6	95.5
Nonrelatives						
Roomer/boarder	0.4	2.1	2.2	0.1	0.8	0.9
Patient/resident[e]	2.2	1.0	2.9	2.5	2.1	2.3
Other	0.4	2.1	0.7	0.7	0.4	1.3
Subtotal	3.0	5.2	5.8	3.3	3.3	4.5
N	5,947	194	545	7,896	238	744

Table 5-1 is continued on the next page.

Table 5-1. Percent in Selected Relationships to Head of Household by Sex, Ethnicity,[a] Cohort, and Census Year (continued)

	Men (Percent)			*Women (Percent)*		
Relationship	*W*	*H*	*AA*	*W*	*H*	*AA*
COHORT B, 1990 (Ages 75 to 84)						
Relatives						
Head/spouse	91.8	78.7	84.7	84.3	64.9	79.7
Child[b]	0.0	0.1	0.0	0.0	0.1	0.1
Parent[c]	1.6	9.7	3.3	4.6	16.3	7.7
Sibling[d]	0.7	0.8	1.4	1.5	1.8	2.6
Other	1.1	5.5	2.3	2.5	11.1	3.9
Subtotal	95.2	94.8	91.7	92.9	94.2	94.0
Nonrelatives						
Roomer/boarder	0.2	0.3	1.4	0.2	0.8	0.4
Patient/resident[e]	3.7	2.7	5.2	6.2	3.5	4.6
Other	0.8	2.3	1.7	0.6	1.5	1.0
Subtotal	4.7	5.3	8.3	7.0	5.8	6.0
N	35,529	1,170	2,596	58,563	1,860	4,774
COHORT C, 1960 (Ages 35 to 44)						
Relatives						
Head/spouse	90.2	80.4	81.3	92.7	86.4	85.4
Child[b]	5.1	4.7	7.4	4.8	7.3	7.4
Parent[c]	0.0	0.5	0.1	0.1	0.5	0.4
Sibling[d]	1.1	3.7	2.1	0.6	1.8	1.1
Other	0.2	1.4	0.2	0.3	0.5	0.9
Subtotal	96.6	90.7	91.0	98.5	96.5	95.2
Nonrelatives						
Roomer/boarder	1.1	1.4	4.7	0.5	1.8	3.0
Patient/resident[e]	1.2	0.9	3.1	0.4	0.5	0.7
Other	1.1	7.0	1.1	0.6	1.4	1.0
Subtotal	3.4	9.3	8.9	1.5	3.7	4.7
N	10,386	214	1,061	10,955	220	1,242

Table 5-1 is continued on the next page.

Table 5-1. Percent in Selected Relationships to Head of Household by Sex, Ethnicity,[a] Cohort, and Census Year (continued)

	Men (Percent)			*Women (Percent)*		
Relationship	*W*	*H*	*AA*	*W*	*H*	*AA*
COHORT C, 1970 (Ages 45 to 54)						
Relatives						
Head/spouse	94.2	90.3	84.1	93.6	90.8	86.4
Child[b]	2.5	2.9	5.1	2.7	1.3	4.2
Parent[c]	0.1	1.8	0.7	0.7	3.8	2.7
Sibling[d]	1.0	1.2	2.6	1.2	1.1	2.6
Other	0.1	0.6	1.3	0.1	1.1	0.5
Subtotal	97.9	96.8	93.8	98.3	98.1	96.4
Nonrelatives						
Roomer/boarder	0.7	0.6	3.1	0.5	0.3	1.8
Patient/resident[e]	0.9	1.2	1.6	0.4	0.5	0.8
Other	0.6	1.5	1.5	0.8	1.1	1.2
Subtotal	2.2	3.3	6.2	1.7	1.9	3.8
N	9,784	340	936	10,358	371	1,129
COHORT C, 1980 (Ages 55 to 64)						
Relatives						
Head/spouse	95.5	89.6	84.0	93.8	85.2	87.9
Child[b]	0.9	0.9	2.3	1.0	0.0	2.0
Parent[c]	0.5	3.6	1.8	1.8	8.7	3.8
Sibling[d]	0.9	1.5	3.1	1.5	2.5	1.7
Other	0.2	0.3	1.1	0.1	1.1	1.4
Subtotal	98.0	95.9	92.3	98.2	97.5	96.8
Nonrelatives						
Roomer/boarder	0.4	1.2	2.1	0.2	0.5	1.2
Patient/resident[e]	1.0	1.5	2.2	1.0	0.8	0.6
Other	0.6	1.5	3.3	0.6	1.1	1.5
Subtotal	2.0	4.2	7.6	1.8	2.4	3.2
N	8,680	337	813	9,883	366	1,087

Table 5-1 is continued on the next page.

Table 5-1. Percent in Selected Relationships to Head of Household by Sex, Ethnicity,[a] Cohort, and Census Year (continued)

	Men (Percent)			*Women (Percent)*		
Relationship	*W*	*H*	*AA*	*W*	*H*	*AA*
COHORT C, 1990 (Ages 65 to 74)						
Relatives						
Head/spouse	95.3	85.8	87.6	92.9	72.9	88.2
Child[b]	0.2	0.2	0.6	0.3	0.3	0.5
Parent[c]	0.8	4.8	1.8	2.2	12.8	4.4
Sibling[d]	0.7	1.2	1.7	1.0	2.5	1.8
Other	0.6	4.4	1.9	1.2	7.2	1.9
Subtotal	97.6	96.4	93.6	97.6	95.7	96.8
Nonrelatives						
Roomer/boarder	0.3	0.5	1.2	0.1	0.6	0.4
Patient/resident[e]	1.3	1.2	2.7	1.5	0.7	1.6
Other	0.8	1.9	2.5	0.8	3.0	1.2
Subtotal	2.4	3.6	6.4	2.4	4.3	3.2
N	73,858	1,292	5,716	93,317	1,889	8,267

Source: Computed from Public Use Samples, 1960, 1970, 1980, 1990
[a]For this and all tables, ethnic groups are represented by W=white, H=Hispanic, and AA=African American.
[b]Respondent is the child, stepchild, or son/daughter-in-law of the head of the household.
[c]Respondent is the parent, stepparent, or father/mother-in-law of the head of the householder.
[d]Respondent is sibling, stepsibling, or brother/sister-in-law of the head of the household.
[e]Respondent is a patient or resident in a nursing home, domiciliary care facility, mental institution, prison, or any other group living arrangement.

The effects of these changes on intergender and interethnic comparisons are seen best in table 5-2, which demonstrates that most, but not all, groups have smaller numbers of people living as head of household or spouse of head as their cohorts age. This holds more universally true for the two older cohorts, and describes three of the six ethnic-gender combinations in Cohort C as well. Still, the groups do not lose this status at the same rate. For example, in every ethnic group, men lose this status at a lower rate than women (or, as in the case of African Americans in Cohort C, gain this status at a higher rate). Within gender categories, Hispanics tend to lose this status much more rapidly than either African Americans or whites.

As a result of this differential loss, older Hispanics experience a kind of "double jeopardy" of losing their status as head of household.

It should be noted that Hispanics (or at least major groups within the heterogeneous cultures combined in this volume under the general heading Hispanic) may not value independence or even household headship in older years as much as other ethnic groups do. Research by Markides et al. (1983) suggests that older Hispanic women expect to live with their children, but it is not clear whether they prefer the extended family arrangement (Tienda and Angel, 1982). Thus, to speak of jeopardy for this group to have the "less desired" housing status may not reflect the subjective experience of Hispanics. By the same token, it is not impossible that the strong extended family is embraced as a value by Hispanic families, in part, because it is a financial necessity. An additional complicating factor is the likelihood that immigrant Hispanic elders are more dependent on their children in the United States (because of language and other adjustment factors) than they would have been in their country of origin (Biafora and Longino, 1990.)

African American women have the opposite experience from Hispanic women. Their losses of head/spouse status are smaller than whites (or in the case of Cohort C, their gains are larger), so that they experience a leveling effect. For example, in Cohort A, African American women were about 90 percent as likely as white women to be household head/spouse. When this group reached ages 65 to 74 in 1970, they were nearly 94 percent as likely, and in the next 20 years they were about 96 percent as likely. These differences are small, and those for African American men are even smaller and less unidirectional, but the overall trend among men is also toward leveling.

Other Noninstitutional Living Arrangements

But what of those in who are not heads of household or spouses of heads? What are their living arrangements? This is also shown in table 5-1. For whites, and even more for Hispanics and African Americans, the largest remaining group lives in a household headed by one of their relatives. Although there is fluctuation in the younger ages, all ethnic groups show an increased proportion living in this arrangement as they age beyond 55 to 64 to 65 to 74 in Cohorts A and B. In Cohort C, four of the six ethnic-gender groups show this same pattern.

Hispanic women are the group most likely to live in a family member's home, and white men are the least likely. This pattern holds for 11 of the 12 cohort-year observation points. (The exception is for the youngest group, Cohort C in 1960.)

In fact, women are more often found in this arrangement than men of their own race for ages 55 and older in all cohorts. This is true in all three census years. White elders are less likely to live in a relative's home than either Hispanics or African Americans. Hispanics are, in general, more likely. This is, however, a more consistent pattern for women. Among men, African American men were more likely to live with relatives in the younger ages, and Hispanic men in the older ones. There are a number of possible explanations for this ethnic difference, including cultures that have a tradition of extended families (Tienda and Angel, 1982), economic necessity (Tienda and Angel, 1982), earlier aging of the minority elderly (Bengtson, 1979), and earlier widowhood of the minority elderly (U.S. Bureau of the Census, 1982).

Table 5-2. Percentage Change in Proportion with Most Desirable Living Status by Cohort, Ethnicity,[a] and Sex

	Men (Percent Change)			*Women (Percent Change)*		
Years	*W*	*H*	*AA*	*W*	*H*	*AA*
COHORT A						
1960–70	0.7	−10.8	− 0.2	− 2.1	−12.7	1.7
1970–80	− 4.0	− 1.5	− 6.5	−11.1	−11.6	− 9.0
1980–90	−13.2	−16.7	− 9.6	−20.2	−30.0	−20.2
1960–90	−16.1	−26.8	−15.7	−30.5	−46.0	−26.2
COHORT B						
1960–70	2.2	3.4	3.5	−0.5	− 4.9	1.1
1970–80	−0.2	− 3.8	4.1	−1.0	−10.0	−1.2
1980–90	−2.1	− 9.6	−4.6	−6.1	−13.7	−4.6
1960–90	−0.2	−10.1	2.8	−7.6	−26.2	−4.7
COHORT C						
1960–70	4.4	12.3	3.4	1.0	5.1	1.2
1970–80	1.4	−0.8	−0.1	0.2	− 6.2	1.7
1980–90	−0.2	−4.2	4.3	−1.0	−14.4	0.3
1960–90	5.7	6.7	7.7	0.2	−15.6	3.3

Table 5-2 is continued on the next page.

Table 5-2. Percentage Change in Proportion with Most Desirable Living Status by Cohort, Ethnicity,[a] and Sex (continued)

	Men (Ratio)		*Women (Ratio)*	
Years	*AA/W*	*H/W*	*AA/W*	*H/W*
COHORT A				
1960	0.930	0.980	0.902	0.927
1970	0.921	0.869	0.936	0.826
1980	0.898	0.892	0.959	0.822
1990	0.935	0.856	0.958	0.720
COHORT B				
1960	0.896	0.951	0.917	0.964
1970	0.907	0.963	0.932	0.922
1980	0.947	0.929	0.930	0.837
1990	0.923	0.857	0.945	0.770
COHORT C				
1960	0.901	0.891	0.921	0.932
1970	0.893	0.959	0.923	0.970
1980	0.880	0.938	0.937	0.908
1990	0.919	0.900	0.949	0.785

Source: Computed from Public Use Samples, 1960, 1970, 1980, 1990

[a]For this and all tables, ethnic groups are represented by W=white, H=Hispanic, and AA=African American.

Minority elders in general, and African American men in particular, are more likely than whites to live with nonrelatives. Although the proportions are small, African American men are especially more likely than other groups to live in boarding or rooming house arrangements.

Group Quarters and Institutions

The proportion of adults living in group quarters or institutions (primarily nursing homes) remains very small until age 85 and older, though for most groups the risk increases for all ages over 55. At age 85, 14 percent of white men and around 10 percent of Hispanic and African American men were in these types of quarters. Hispanic women were only a little more likely to live in institutions than their male counterparts, 11 percent. However, 15 percent of African American women and 23 percent of white women were doing so.

Table 5-3 Percentage Change in Proportion in Group Quarters/Institutions by Sex, Cohort, and Ethnicity[a]

	Men (Percent Change)			*Women (Percent Change)*		
Years	*W*	*H*	*AA*	*W*	*H*	*AA*
Cohort A						
1960–70	31.3	83.3	180.0	38.5	—	- 15.8
1970–80	166.7	30.3	317.9	438.9	40.0	281.3
1980–90	150.0	125.6	- 13.8	140.6	423.8	149.0
1960–90	775.0	438.9	909.0	1,695.4	—	699.5
Cohort B						
1960–70	7.1	0.0	4.5	0.0	—	- 30.8
1970–80	46.7	- 28.6	26.1	177.8	—	155.6
1980–90	68.2	170.0	79.3	148.0	66.7	100.0
1960–90	164.3	92.9	136.4	588.9	—	253.8
Cohort C						
1960–70	–25.0	33.3	–48.4	0.0	0.0	14.3
1970–80	11.1	25.0	37.5	150.0	60.0	- 25.0
1980–90	30.0	–20.0	22.7	50.0	–12.5	166.7
1960–90	8.3	33.3	–12.9	275.0	40.0	128.6

	Men (Ratio)		*Women (Ratio)*	
Years	*AA/W*	*H/W*	*AA/W*	*H/W*
Cohort A				
1960	0.625	1.125	1.462	0.000
1970	1.333	1.571	0.889	0.833
1980	0.344	0.768	0.629	0.216
1990	0.721	0.693	0.651	0.471
Cohort B				
1960	1.571	1.000	1.444	0.000
1970	1.533	0.933	1.000	0.000
1980	1.318	0.455	0.920	0.840
1990	1.405	0.730	0.742	0.565
Cohort C				
1960	2.583	0.750	1.750	1.250
1970	1.778	1.333	2.000	1.250
1980	2.200	1.500	0.600	0.800
1990	2.077	0.923	1.067	0.467

Source: Computed from Public Use Sample 1960, 1970, 1980, 1990

[a]For this and all tables, ethnic groups are represented by W=white, H=Hispanic, and AA=African American.

There is a large variation among age-cohort and gender-ethnicity groups in their likelihood of institutionalization. In general, in the ages before retirement, minority elders were more likely to be in group or institutional settings than whites, but for all ages 65 and older whites are more likely than other groups. As shown in table 5-3, African American men have a greater likelihood of this living arrangement than white men in three-quarters (9 of 12) of the age-cohort groups represented. African American women are more likely to live in institutions than white women in half of the age points, largely concentrated in the younger ages. Hispanic men were more likely to live in institutions than white men less than half of the time and always in the younger ages, but Hispanic women were more likely to live in institutions than white women in only two of the 12 ages (the two youngest points in the youngest cohort).

Cohort Comparisons

A comparison of the three cohorts shows that they are not very different, and that age does not seem to have a very large effect until the oldest ages (75 to 84 and 85+). When comparing cohorts at the same age (e.g., Cohort A in 1960 with Cohort B in 1970 with Cohort C in 1980), respondents from younger cohorts are slightly more likely to live as head/spouse at each age for the preponderance of ethnic-gender groups. This relationship is underscored by the greater likelihood that people from the older cohorts are more likely to live with relatives across the age and ethnic-gender groups. Rates of institutionalization are uniformly low across cohorts until age 75 to 84. Among those who have attained that age, five of the six ethnic-gender groups have higher rates in Cohort A than in Cohort B. Across all cohorts, whites are the most likely group to have *both* the most desirable arrangement (head of household) and the least desirable (nursing home or other group arrangements) while minority elders, especially Hispanics, are more likely than white elders to live in the homes of family members.

Predictors of Living Arrangement

Assuming a hierarchy of desirable living arrangements with independent living (head or spouse) rated 3, living with a relative rated 2, living with a nonrelative rated 1, and living in an institution rated 0, a multiple regression equation can be estimated for each cohort 65 or older, using desirability of living arrangements as the dependent variable. The parameter estimates are quite small, because, as we have seen, most people live in the most desired arrangement. However, some of these small differences are significant. The results are presented in table 5-4.

Table 5-4. Significance Levels for Predictors of Desirable Living Arrangements for People Aged 65 or Older

Variables	*1970*	*1980*	*1990*
COHORT A	*Ages 65 to 74*	*Ages 75 to 84*	*Ages 85+*
African American	–.0009	—	.0001
Hispanic	–.0001	—	.0291
Education	.0001	—	.0009
Wed	.0001	.0001	.0001
Own home	–.0001	.0001	.0001
Family income	–.0001	–.0001	–.0001
Low occupation	–.0001	–.0001	–.0001
South	—	–.0085	–.0001
R^2	.1769	.1592	.2743
COHORT B	Not	*Ages 65 to 74*	*Ages 75 to 84*
African American	Applicable	—	.0004
Hispanic		—	–.0002
Education		.0001	.0001
Wed		.0001	.0001
Own home		.0001	.0001
Family income		–.0001	–.0001
Low occupation		–.0001	–.0001
South		—	–.0001
R^2		.1179	.1400
COHORT C	Not	Not	*Ages 65 to 74*
African American	Applicable	Applicable	—
Hispanic			–.0001
Education			.0001
Wed			.0001
Own home			.0001
Family income			–.0001
Low occupation			–.0001
South			—
R^2			.0948

Source: Computed from Public Use Samples, 1960, 1970, 1980, 1990

With other variables controlled, the effect of ethnicity per se varies with age and cohort. At age 65 to 74, the effect of ethnicity on desirable living arrangements is either negative (both ethnicities in Cohort A and Hispanic ethnicity in Cohort C) or not significant. At ages 75 to 84 ethnicity is not significant for Cohort A. In Cohort B at these ages, it is positive for African Americans and negative for Hispanics. At age 85 and older, reached only by Cohort A, the effect of both ethnicities was positive. The change from negative to positive in Cohort A may reflect the changing distribution of the dependent variable as the risk of nursing home placement increased. However there is no immediate interpretation of the intercohort variations.

The variables that remain consistent over time and cohort are marital status (+), low occupation (–), and family income (–). The negative "effect" of family income on living arrangement is actually a *result* of living arrangement, because the earnings of younger relatives are part of the family income of those who live with relatives while those who live independently have only retirement income to show. The effect of occupation here is probably largely the effect of employment rather than occupation per se. Since retired/unemployed are coded lower than the lowest occupational category, being retired from any job will score lower than working at any job.

Number of Older Adults in the Home

Another census variable that can provide some information about ethnic variations in the living arrangements of older adults appeared in the 1960 and 1970 Public Use Samples of the Census: "The number of persons 65 or older in the household." This ignores the question of headship and identifies cases where people of working age have people in the household who are past the traditional retirement age. It is necessary to remember in interpreting these data that for the group ages 55 to 64, a substantial number of the "older" people in the household may be spouses rather than parents.

Table 5-5, which shows the distribution of this variable for the three cohorts, indicates no ethnic differences, but does show some age and cohort differences in the likelihood that people younger than 65 will have someone over 65 living with them. As expected from table 5-1, which shows that most older people live as heads of household or spouses of head, most middle-aged people do not have older people living with them. Comparing cohorts at the same age, that is Cohorts A and B at ages 55 to 64, and Cohorts B and C at ages 45 to 54, indicates that more recent cohorts are less likely to have a person over 65 living with them than people the same age in earlier cohorts.

Table 5-5. Number of People 65+ in the Household for the Population Aged 64 and Younger, by Ethnicity[a] and Cohort

People 65+ in Household	*1960* W	*1960* H	*1960* AA	*1970* W	*1970* H	*1970* AA
COHORT A		*Ages 55 to 64*			*Ages 65 to 74*	
0	79.3	79.9	8.4			
1	19.0	19.2	19.3		Not Applicable	
2	1.5	0.5	2.2			
3+	0.1	0.5	0.1			
N	14,061	198	1,225			
COHORT B		*Ages 45 to 54*			*Ages 55 to 64*	
0	87.8	86.2	87.2	81.2	81.2	81.1
1	10.6	12.7	11.1	17.7	16.9	17.2
2	1.4	1.1	1.5	1.1	1.9	1.3
3+	0.1	0.0	0.2	0.1	0.0	0.4
N	18,396	276	1,829	16,566	425	1,634
COHORT C		*Ages 35 to 44*			*Ages 45 to 54*	
0	91.0	92.6	90.9	90.5	87.9	89.1
1	7.4	6.0	7.8	8.2	10.5	8.8
2	1.5	1.4	1.3	1.2	1.5	1.9
3+	0.1	0.0	0.0	0.0	0.0	0.2
N	21,341	434	2,303	20,142	711	2,065

Source: Computed from Public Use Samples, 1960 and 1970

[a]For this and all tables, ethnic groups are represented by W=white, H=Hispanic, and AA=African American.

The data suggest that within a single cohort, the age group 45 to 54 is the peak time for living with one or more people over 65. However, with only two comparison years (comparing ages 45 to 54 with ages 55 to 64 in cohort B and ages 45 to 54 with ages 35 to 54 in Cohort C), it is not safe to generalize very far. The likelihood of a middle-aged adult of any given age sharing living arrangements with a person over 65 is a function of both the older person's ability to maintain independence (financially and physically) and the childbearing history of the older person (given that the majority of people over 65 living with relatives are living with children or grandchildren). As the period of childbearing becomes more condensed while the functional life expectancy and financial well-being of older adults increases, it is hard to predict what changes this may create in the ages in which adult children are most likely to share homes with their frail parents .

It is interesting to note that while older Hispanics are more likely than whites or African Americans to live with their children, middle-aged Hispanics are not more likely than African Americans or whites to have people over 65 in their homes. This may be related to a larger number of children ever born, which would distribute the probability of a parent moving in over a larger number of families. On the other hand, it may be related to the large number of first-generation immigrants among younger Hispanics who have no older generation living in the United States.

Because of the desirability of the older person living independently, from the perspective of either the older person or the offspring, demographic variables are not very good predictors of the number of people over 65 living in the home (when younger people are the subjects). The mental and physical health of the older person and the availability of home services are just two of the nondemographic factors that could be expected to be better predictors.

Nevertheless, multiple regression equations fitted to the younger cohorts in this study do reveal some very small but statistically significant predictors of the number of older people living with young respondents. In this analysis, only respondents age 35 to 44 (Cohort C in 1960) and 45 to 54 (Cohort B in 1960 and Cohort C in 1970) were used. This decision was made to eliminate confusion in the 55 to 64 age group between older parents and slightly older spouses who would be counted together. A new variable, *crowded*, was created for this analysis. It was computed by subtracting any people over 65 from the total number of people in the household, and then dividing the remaining (younger) people by the number of bedrooms in the household. This should prove indicative of the ability to house older relatives. Table 5-6 shows the estimates from this analysis.

No clear role of ethnicity in determining living arrangements emerges from this analysis. The variables African American and Hispanic were negatively related to older adults in the household for Cohort C at ages 35 to 44, positively related for Cohort C at ages 45 to

54, and not significantly related at all for Cohort B at ages 45 to 54. It is extremely hard to interpret these data. What does emerge is that currently single people (includes never married, divorced, and widowed) with high family incomes and a low ratio of people to bedrooms are consistently more likely than others to have older people in their homes, and that these factors are more consistent predictors than ethnicity across the groups in this study. It is worth noting that these predictors make good economic sense but are in general disagreement with literary/media stereotypes that present the large, poor sprawling family as having room for Grandma, while the cold, middle-class small family puts their grandmother in an institution.

Table 5-6. Significance Levels for Predictors of the Number of People Aged 65 and Older Living in the Home, for Cohorts B and C, in 1960 and 1970

Variables	*Cohort B 1960 45 to 54*	*Cohort C 1970 35 to 44*	*Cohort C 1980 45 to 54*
African American	—	–.0023	.0262
Hispanic	—	–.0433	.0001
Education	—	–.0001	–.0001
Married	–.0001	–.0001	–.0001
Own home	.0001	.0001	.0001
Family income	.0007	.0001	.0001
Occupation	–.0416	—	–.0005
South	—	—	—
Crowded	–.0001	–.0001	–.0001
R^2	.0594	.1107	.0657

Source: Computed from Public Use Samples, 1960, 1970, 1980

Home Ownership

Owning a home provides a large sector of the population with its most valuable economic asset. For the older adult, it is an asset in two respects. It provides rent-free housing, and its equity can frequently be converted to cash in emergencies. This, then, is an asset beyond family income that must be considered in comparing the financial well-being of ethnic groups, especially among older adults.

Table 5-7 shows that this asset is distributed in somewhat the same way as family income. At every age and in every census year, whites are more likely than African Americans or Hispanics to live in houses they own. However, the ethnic differences in home ownership are not exactly analogous to the differences in family income. Older Hispanics have median incomes approximately midway between those of whites and African Americans across time and cohorts. However, the proportions of Hispanics owning their homes across time are, in general, much close to the proportions of African Americans than of whites.

Table 5-7. Percentage of All People Who Are Living as Head of Household (or Spouse of Head) in Houses They Own, by Ethnicity,[a] Cohort, and Year

	Percent			*Ratio*	
Year (Age)	*W*	*H*	*AA*	*AA/W*	*H/W*
COHORT A					
1960 (55–64)	64.8	46.5	42.9	0.662	0.718
1970 (65–74)	64.1	45.5	43.8	0.683	0.710
1980 (75–84)	55.8	42.6	43.1	0.772	0.763
1990 (85+)	44.5	29.7	40.9	0.919	0.667
COHORT B					
1960 (45–54)	67.6	43.8	39.9	0.590	0.648
1970 (55–64)	71.2	52.9	47.4	0.666	0.743
1980 (65–74)	72.2	45.8	55.5	0.769	0.634
1990 (75–84)	68.3	43.0	54.7	0.801	0.630
COHORT C					
1960 (35–44)	66.2	40.3	33.3	0.503	0.609
1970 (45–54)	74.4	54.6	47.4	0.637	0.734
1980 (55–64)	79.9	55.3	56.0	0.701	0.692
1990 (65–74)	80.8	46.0	61.0	0.755	0.569

Source: Computed from Public Use Samples, 1960, 1970, 1980, 1990

[a]For this and all tables, ethnic groups are represented by W=white, H=Hispanic, and AA=African American.

There are at least three factors at work to make this so: (1) like African Americans, Hispanics are much more likely than whites to live in central cities, where much of the available housing is in multifamily rental units; (2) like African Americans, Hispanics have faced housing discrimination; and (3) although Hispanics have higher average incomes, this is offset by cultural barriers that may prevent them from seeking programs designed to provide housing for lower-income people (Hoover, 1981).

The two groups are *not* similar in the changes in their ownership over time, relative to whites. African Americans experience leveling in this variable. This is observable in the two right columns of table 5-7. For example, in Cohort A, 64.8 percent of 55- to 65-year-old whites lived as head (or spouse of head) in a home they own. Only 42.9 percent of African Americans had this arrangement, or about 66.2 percent the rate for whites of the same age. At ages 65 to 74, African Americans were 68 percent as likely to own homes, and at ages 75 to 84, 77 percent. Finally, in 1990, when the cohort reached ages 75 to 84, African Americans were about 92 percent as likely as whites. This leveling, like that shown by other variables, was due to substantially greater losses among whites to own homes.

A more detailed breakdown of home ownership shows that the increase of whites in "group quarters" at the oldest age is primarily at the expense of heads or spouses who own their home, while the increase of African Americans in that category is largely drawn from the group who had been heads or spouses paying cash rent, thus accounting for leveling in the home ownership variable. Cohorts B and C also demonstrate leveling for African Americans, but in these cases it is due to greater gains in home ownership for African Americans rather than greater losses for whites.

Changes for Hispanics in this arrangement sometimes mirror those for whites and sometimes do not. As a result, there is fluctuation in the numbers of Hispanics living as head of their own home relative to whites, but there is no pattern in this fluctuation.

When cohorts are compared across the same age groups, it is clear that at any given age the more recent cohorts not only have higher incomes but are also more likely to own their own homes than were people of the same ethnic group in earlier cohorts at that age. For example, (as discussed above) when Cohort A was ages 55 to 64 in 1960, 65 percent of whites, 47 percent of Hispanics, and 43 percent of African Americans owned their homes. In 1970, when Cohort B was 55 to 64, 71 percent of whites, 53 percent of Hispanics, and 47 percent of African Americans owned homes. In 1980, when Cohort C was 55 to 64, the corresponding figures were 80 percent of whites, 55 percent of

Hispanics, and 56 percent of African Americans. As this shows, more recent cohorts fare better than earlier ones, regardless of ethnicity, but ethnic groups are not any closer to equity in more recent cohorts than in earlier ones.

Assets and Resources beyond Home Ownership: A Period Analysis

These data do not provide information about wealth or assets, with the exception of recording home ownership as discussed above. However, the March 1980 Current Population Survey does document income from assets. This can serve as a proxy for assets of the elderly at a single point in time. It does not permit the longitudinal analysis necessary to test double jeopardy directly, but it does allow some suggestive period comparisons.

Who Receives Income from Assets?

Table 5-8 shows the distribution of income from wages, pensions, and assets, by ethnicity, for the three cohorts in 1980. The three ethnic groups are very similar in the number receiving some income from wages in each age/cohort category. Whites are more likely to have private pensions (15 and 19 percent in Cohorts A and B, compared to 8 percent and 9 percent for Hispanics and 6 percent and 11 percent for African Americans). While the younger retired cohort has higher percentages receiving pensions within each ethnic group, the magnitude of ethnic differences is very similar across cohorts.

There are only three sources of income that are more prevalent among minority elders than among white ones at any point in time—railroad retirement, alimony/child support, and contributions from family members. It is important to note that these are all sources that affect very small numbers of people in these ages, regardless of ethnicity.

It is in the existence of income from *assets*, more than *pensions*, that the clear advantage of the white group is most evident. In Cohort B (65 to 74), for example, 72 percent of whites had some income from interest, compared to 37 percent of Hispanics and 28 percent of African Americans. Some 17 percent of whites had income from dividends, compared to 4 percent of Hispanics and 1 percent of African Americans; 11 percent of whites had income from rents or royalties, compared to 7 percent of Hispanics and African Americans.

Table 5-8. Percent with Personal Income from Nongovernmental Sources in 1980, by Source, Ethnicity,[a] and Age/Cohort

	Percent			*Ratio*	
Source of Income	*W*	*H*	*AA*	*AA/W*	*H/W*
COHORT A, (Ages 75 to 84)					
Wages	6.2	3.3	5.0	0.806	0.532
Self-employed	2.0	1.9	1.2	0.600	0.950
Farm income	0.9	0.5	0.5	0.556	0.556
Railroad retirement	2.9	2.8	4.1	1.414	0.966
Interest	70.3	27.9	21.7	0.309	0.397
Dividends	14.8	2.8	0.5	0.034	0.189
Rents and royalties	11.5	7.9	7.6	0.661	0.687
Estates and trusts	1.4	0.5	0.0	0.000	0.357
Private pensions	14.6	7.9	5.7	0.390	0.541
Alimony/child support	0.2	0.0	0.0	0.000	0.000
Family contributions	0.4	0.5	0.0	0.000	1.250
Other nongovernment	1.2	0.0	0.7	0.583	0.000
N	4,492	215	419		
COHORT B, (Ages 65 to 74)					
Wages	19.0	18.8	22.3	1.174	0.989
Self-employed	4.1	3.5	1.8	0.439	0.854
Farm income	2.0	0.6	0.3	0.150	0.300
Railroad retirement	2.3	2.5	2.2	0.957	1.087
Interest	72.0	36.6	27.7	0.385	0.508
Dividends	16.9	3.7	1.3	0.077	0.219
Rents and royalties	11.4	7.2	6.6	0.579	0.632
Estates and trusts	1.4	0.4	0.2	0.143	0.286
Private pensions	19.2	8.6	10.7	0.557	0.448
Alimony/child support	0.1	0.0	0.0	0.000	0.000
Family contributions	0.2	0.6	0.3	1.500	3.000
Other nongovernment	1.4	0.6	0.4	0.286	0.429
N	10,363	511	975		

Table 5-8 is continued on the next page.

Table 5-8. Percent with Personal Income from Nongovernmental Sources in 1980, by Source, Ethnicity,[a] and Age/Cohort (continued)

	Percent			*Ratio*	
Source of Income	*W*	*H*	*AA*	*AA/W*	*H/W*
COHORT C (Ages 55 to 64)					
Wages	54.2	52.2	53.4	0.985	0.963
Self-employed	7.9	6.1	3.4	0.430	0.772
Farm income	3.2	0.6	0.4	0.125	0.188
Railroad retirement	0.6	1.0	0.7	1.167	1.667
Interest	69.9	42.0	27.4	0.392	0.601
Dividends	17.8	5.0	1.3	0.073	0.281
Rents and royalties	11.4	7.1	6.6	0.579	0.623
Estates and trusts	1.4	0.8	0.2	0.143	0.571
Private pensions	6.9	4.5	4.4	0.638	0.652
Alimony/child support	0.3	0.5	0.3	1.000	1.667
Family contributions	0.2	0.6	0.5	2.500	3.000
Other nongovernment	1.5	0.7	1.2	0.800	0.467
N	14,405	864	1,308		

Source: Computed from March 1980 Current Population Survey
[a]For this and all tables, ethnic groups are represented by W=white, H=Hispanic, and AA=African American.

How Much Income Do Older Adults Receive from Assets?

Whites are not only more likely to receive income from interest and dividends than African Americans or Hispanics, but they also receive a higher median income from these sources[5] (see table 5-9). Half of the whites in Cohort A who had income from interest received $524 per year or less. The median for Hispanics in Cohort A is $375 and that of African Americans is $100. For the young elderly of Cohort B, the numbers are smaller, but very similar. Whites had a median income from interest of $500; Hispanics, $100; and African Americans, $80.

Fewer people have dividends, but income for those who do is higher than that for interest. For whites in Cohort A who have income from dividends, the median is $867. For Hispanics the median is $1,075,[6] and for African Americans it is $560.

Table 5-9. Median Annual Household Income in 1980 from Selected Nongovernmental Sources, by Source, Age, and Ethnicity[a]

	W		*H*		*AA*	
Sources	*Median*	N	*Median*	N	*Median*	N
COHORT A (Ages 75 to 84)						
Wages	$2,398	307	$2,790	7	$2,340	21
Self-employment	1,536	101	3,000	4	150	5
Farm income	1,700	47	2,400	1	1,000	2
Interest	524	3,508	375	60	100	91
Dividend	867	1,217	1075	24	560	34
Private pension	2,285	1,187	1,810	23	2,565	42
Family[b]	500	80	300	1	200	3
COHORT B (Ages 65 to 74)						
Wages	$3,805	1,970	$4,000	96	$2,400	217
Self-employment	2,459	428	1,476	18	700	18
Farm income	3,000	210	1,000	3	1,000	3
Interest	500	7,458	100	187	80	270
Dividend	600	2,697	531	54	500	75
Private Pension	2,600	2,995	3,000	68	3,529	176
Family[b]	480	173	1,297	6	500	7

Source: Computed from March 1980 Current Population Survey

[a]For this and all tables, ethnic groups are represented by W=white, H=Hispanic, and AA=African American.

[b]Includes alimony, child support, and regular contributions from family members.

Since all figures in this table apply to the same year, they are not converted to constant dollars. Readers wishing to compare these amounts with data for 1990 may compute constant 1990 dollars by multiplying the 1980 amount by 1.5862.

How does this influence double jeopardy? As far as the widening or narrowing of ethnic differences in assets over the life course, these data cannot answer that question. However, there are implications of these ethnic differences. Given that most retired people depend for income on Social Security, other pensions (a small percentage in these cohorts as seen in table 5-8), and their assets; and given that both entitlement and amount of Social Security are relatively similar among ethnic groups (see the discussion below); ethnic differences in assets should influence the direction of income equity. The amounts of interest and dividends discussed here are *not* enough to cause double jeopardy of income. The jeopardy they do represent is in financial security for unforeseen needs.

The annual income difference made by $500 in interest compared to $100 in interest is very small. However, the difference in the size of bank accounts that generate $500 interest per year and those which generate $100 per year may be very important. Hence, there is reason to believe that differences in assets, as well as in home ownership, represent a sort of jeopardy of vulnerability.[7]

Government Transfer Payments

These data fail to provide data on two major government expenditure for the elderly—Medicare and tax expenditures. In 1982, the federal government spent more than $41.5 billion on Medicare reimbursements (Health Care Financing Administration, 1985), and $43.7 billion on tax expenditures for older adults (revenue forgone by the government due to exemptions and deductions; Nelson, 1983). These two taken together represent only about 55 percent of 1982's expenditure for Social Security (OASDI),[8] but each separately is almost as large as the sum of civil service pensions, veteran's pensions, and public assistance (for all ages) in that year.[9] Effects of neither Medicare nor tax expenditures can be measured using these data, and expenditures are not published by race. Medicare *may* be paid to the poor disproportionately (and thus, disproportionately to minorities) because their health is worse. It is almost certainly of more value to the poor, who are more vulnerable to the loss of all resources with a long illness. In this sense it represents a sort of leveling of opportunity. Tax expenditures, on the other hand, fall heavily on the wealthy (Nelson, 1983), and thus disproportionately to whites. Hence, it is a force against leveling that is not revealed by income data.

While individual receipts from these government expenditures cannot be assessed from the data at hand, a number of important government transfers can be examined. Like assets, they are only presented for one time and thus cannot be used for longitudinal analysis.

Who Receives Money from the Government?

Table 5-10 presents an array of government transfer payments—Social Security, Aid to Dependent Children (ADC), public assistance, veterans' payments, workmen's compensation, military retirement, federal pensions, state/local pensions, other U.S. government payments, and other state/local government payments. It also provides household information on two in-kind programs: subsidized low-income housing and food stamps. Not unexpectedly, the proportion of people receiving these payments varies with both age/cohort and ethnicity.

OASDI (the usual social security retirement benefit) is the direct government payment most commonly associated with older adults, and as table 5-10 shows, the majority of those 65 and older receive these payments, as do a sizable minority of those 55 to 64 (includes early retirement at ages 62 to 64 and widow's benefits). OASDI does *not* benefit the three ethnic groups equally. African Americans, and Hispanics are less likely to receive it than whites (table 5-10), and those who do receive it in both minority groups receive smaller median payments (see table 5-11). Nevertheless, *Social Security and other government programs appear to be the major cause of leveling.* They are the major source of income for older people of all ethnic groups, and the ethnic differences are much smaller than those in income for the preretirement ages.

Table 5-10. Percent with Personal Income from Government Sources, by Source, Ethnicity,[a] and Cohort

	Percent Receiving Income		
Source	*W*	*H*	*AA*
COHORT A (Ages 75 to 84)			
OASDI	91.7	74.9	81.6
ADC	0.0	0.0	0.7
Public assistance	1.1	1.9	3.3
Veterans' payments	5.1	3.3	5.7
Unemployment	0.2	0.0	0.0
Workmen's compensation	1.0	0.5	0.0
Military retirement	1.0	0.0	1.0
Federal pension	3.2	0.9	2.2
State/local pension	5.4	1.9	1.2
Other U.S. government	5.1	23.7	26.5
Other state/local government	2.3	9.3	11.7
Household subsidies			
Rent	6.3	7.4	2.8
Food stamps	4.2	20.0	22.7
N	4,492	215	419

Table 5-10 is continued on the next page.

Table 5-10. Percent with Personal Income from Government Sources, by Source, Ethnicity,[a] and Cohort (continued)

	Percent Receiving Income		
Source	*W*	*H*	*AA*
COHORT B (Ages 65 to 74)			
OASDI	88.2	71.8	81.4
ADC	0.1	0.8	1.1
Public assistance	0.7	2.5	2.4
Veterans' payments	3.5	3.5	4.3
Unemployment	0.9	1.4	0.6
Workmen's compensation	0.9	0.2	0.7
Military retirement	1.1	0.4	0.8
Federal pension	3.2	1.8	3.6
State/local pension	6.4	2.7	3.2
Other U.S. government	3.8	21.5	16.6
Other state/local government	1.6	7.2	6.6
Household subsidies			
Rent	5.7	8.0	6.6
Food stamps	3.8	18.4	22.7
N	10,363	511	975
COHORT C (Ages 55 to 64)			
OASDI	19.7	17.2	24.0
ADC	0.1	2.0	2.2
Public assistance	0.5	2.0	2.4
Veterans' payments	5.8	5.1	5.7
Unemployment	3.6	5.3	3.1
Workmen's compensation	1.8	1.7	1.3
Military retirement	2.0	1.2	1.2
Federal pension	2.1	2.1	2.7
State/local pension	2.2	1.6	1.2
Other U.S. government	1.4	4.3	6.5
Other state/local government	0.6	1.5	3.6
Household subsidies			
Rent	2.1	4.2	3.6
Food stamps	3.0	12.5	20.0
N	14,405	864	1,308

Source: Computed from March 1980 Current Population Survey

[a]For this and all tables, ethnic groups are represented by W=white, H=Hispanic, and AA=African American.

The categories "Other U.S. government" (which includes Supplementary Security Income) and "food stamps" are the major need-based categories covered by these data. They serve a larger proportion of minority than white elderly, and a larger proportion of the elderly than those in late middle age. Recipients of "Other government payments" almost exactly compensate in coverage, though not in amount, for African American and Hispanic elders who do not receive OASDI.

In the three cohorts, 3 to 4 percent of whites received food stamps. In Cohort C 20 percent of African Americans received the stamps, compared to 23 percent of those in the older cohorts. The age difference was slightly larger among Hispanics: 12.5 percent of those in Cohort C, 18.5 percent of those in Cohort B, and 20 percent in Cohort A received food stamps.

Table 5-11. Median Annual Household Income[a] in 1980 from Selected Governmental Sources, by Source, Age, and Ethnicity[b]

	W		*H*		*AA*	
Sources	*Median*	N	*Median*	N	*Median*	N
COHORT A (Ages 75 to 84						
OASDI and pension	$3,164	4,652	$2,340	165	$2,197	350
SSI	916	916	1466	61	973	146
Public assistance	392	58	1,798	4	120	17
Food stamp value	347	212	720	43	456	95
COHORT B (Ages 65 to 74)						
OASDI and pension	$3,120	9,283	$2,367	374	$2,386	804
SSI	870	475	1,078	123	1,111	201
Public assistance	324	77	540	17	714	34
Food stamp value	330	391	583	94	408	221

Source: Computed from March 1980 Current Population Survey

[a]Since all figures in this table apply to the same year, they are not converted to constant dollars. Readers wishing to compare these amounts with data for 1990 may compute constant 1990 dollars by multiplying the 1980 amount by 1.5862.

[b]For this and all tables, ethnic groups are represented by W=white, H=Hispanic, and AA=African American.

Various pensions and welfare payments went to very small numbers of the older adult population (in most cases, less than 5 percent) with larger numbers of whites receiving pension benefits (except veterans' pensions, which African Americans and whites received about with larger numbers of whites receiving pension benefits (except veterans' pensions, which African Americans and whites received about equally) and larger proportions (still very small) of African Americans and Hispanics receiving other need-based aid.

How Do Ethnic Groups Differ in Their Income from Government Payments?

Table 5-11 shows the median household incomes from several categories of government transfers for Cohorts A and B. This table reveals that while whites average higher incomes from Social Security, African Americans and Hispanics receive larger amounts as well as fuller coverage on need-based programs. This again shows that government transfers are a source of leveling, even though the point of leveling is below that of comfort for many older adults.

Summary

Chapter 5 has looked beyond family income as a measure of financial well-being to examine some of the other assets that bring improved life chances and perhaps a greater subjective sense of well-being (though subjective ratings are beyond the scope of this work). This brief overview suggests a reason for the persistence of the double jeopardy hypothesis, even while income figures exhibit income leveling. Not only do older whites fare better than African Americans and Hispanics in income (though not as much better as they did when younger), but they fare better in a number of other ways that add to well-being.

Most older people live as the head of a household or spouse of the head, which is the most desired category. Whites, however, are the most likely to do so at every age. When compared at the same age, younger cohorts are the most likely to live as head or spouse, but ethnic differences are not declining. Hispanics who do not live as head or spouse are more likely than comparable members of other ethnic groups to live with their relatives. This is especially true of Hispanic women. African Americans, especially African American men, who do not have the head/spouse arrangement are more likely than other groups to live with nonrelatives. When other variables are controlled, ethnicity is not a consistently significant predictor of preferred living arrangement.

While there are ethnic differences in the likelihood of an older person living alone, there are no ethnic differences in the likelihood that younger people (35 to 44, and 45 to 54) will have people over 65 living with them. The small but significant demographic predictors of sharing living quarters with an older person are a marital status other than currently married, high income, home ownership, and a low ratio of people younger than 65 per bedroom.

For every cohort/age combination, whites are more likely than African Americans or Hispanics to own their home. For African Americans, these differences decline with age in every cohort, producing a leveling effect. This is not true for older Hispanics. Their home ownership fluctuates somewhat, relative to that of white elders, but there is no distinct pattern of either jeopardy or leveling.

The most dramatic ethnic difference in sources of income comes in income from assets. Whites were much more likely to have income from interest, dividends, and rent than African Americans or Hispanics, and the median amounts received, though not extravagant, were larger for whites than for the other two groups. Although the ethnic differences in the number receiving asset income was not smaller in Cohort B than Cohort A, ethnic differences in the amounts received were slightly smaller in the younger group. Income from assets is an indicator of reserve capital to meet the emergencies that become more common with older age. Therefore this difference, though small in income dollars, is particularly far-reaching in its consequences for financial security.

In data limited to 1980, whites 65 and older were more likely than African Americans and Hispanics to have private pensions, public pensions, and social security. Further, among those who reported income from these sources, whites received higher median payments. (Minority group members were more likely to receive food stamps, subsidized rent, and other need-based payments.) For each ethnic group, the proportion receiving pensions was greater for the younger than the older age group, but the ethnic differences remained nearly constant. Despite the advantages of whites in the area of government transfers, the relatively small differences in amounts and the nearly universal reliance of the elderly population on some form of government transfer as the major source of income made this the major source of leveling.

Notes

[1]In the interest of truth, it is probably just as well not to have such a scale, which would mask a host of assumptions about the relative importance of dissimilar resources behind the artificial precision of a numeric score.

[2]In 1960 and 1970 the husband in a married couple was always coded as the head of household. Women were only listed as heads of household if there was no spouse present. In the 1980 Census, either the husband or wife could be listed as head of household and spouse of head, but only about 3 percent of men were listed as spouse, suggesting that very few married women were listed as head of household.

[3]Married couples are much more likely to remain independent than single individuals, even when both suffer impairment (Weissert, 1984).

[4]These data do not separate wholly owned from mortgaged homes, but national data show that most of the elderly have little or no mortgage on their homes (Sherman, 1985; Pies, 1984)

[5]The median was computed only for those who receive some income from this source.

[6]Only 24 Hispanics in this sample from Cohort A have interest from dividends.

[7]Life insurance and private health insurance supplements to Medicare are additional resources against such vulnerability, but these data sets contain no information about the distribution of these resources.

[8]$155,699,000,000 (Social Security Bulletin, 1985)

[9]

$19,283,900,000	Civil Service Pensions
13,315,400,000	Veteran's Pensions
13,891,800,000	Public Assistance (Social Security Bulletin, 1985)

VI
Summary and a Look To the Future

The arrays of numbers assembled in Chapters 3 through 5 bring us back, ultimately, to those four questions asked in Chapter 1. In light of the cohort data derived from the 1960, 1970, 1980, and 1990 census samples, how can these questions be answered? This chapter will examine each of these in light of the findings reported throughout this book.

The First Question

1. *What were the differences in income and related sociodemographic variables among ethnic groups when the cohorts that are now older adults were in their peak productive years? What variables help explain these differences?*

Chapter 3 examines differences among three cohorts of whites, African Americans, and Hispanics at ages 55 to 64 to answer these questions.

Income

In all three cohorts whites have the highest median family income, and African Americans the lowest. Each successively younger cohort has a higher constant-dollar income at ages 55 to 64 than the cohort preceding it, for each ethnic group taken in turn.

Cohorts B and C show greater equality between African American and white family income than Cohort A, with African American family income less than 50 percent that of white family income in Cohort A and almost 55 percent of white family income in Cohorts B and C. Family income quartiles for that age also show slight gains in white/African American equality from the oldest to the youngest cohort. Despite this improvement, the differences in Cohort C remain quite large—so large, in fact, that the upper limit of the lowest income quartile for whites is greater than the median income for African Americans.

Although Hispanic income consistently falls between white and African American income, its size in relation to white income does not follow a consistent pattern like that of African American to white income. Fluctuation may be due to small sample size or to historical changes in the composition of the Hispanic population. It does not seem to be a function of the changing definition of "Hispanic" between the 1960 and 1970 censuses.

Poverty

Whites are least likely, and African Americans most likely, to have incomes below the poverty level at ages 55 to 64 in both 1970 and 1980. While the proportion below that income level has fallen from cohort to cohort for all three ethnic groups, the relationship between the three remained similar, with Hispanics more than twice as likely, and African Americans more than three times as likely as whites to be in poverty.

Education

Whites are the best educated of the three ethnic groups regardless of the measure chosen. For the most part, African Americans are the worst educated. However, the Hispanic distribution is atypical in two ways: (1) women are less educated than men; and (2) large numbers, especially in the oldest cohort, have no formal education at all. African Americans, by comparison, have fewer high school and college graduates, but more people with some education as opposed to no education.

The educational level is higher for all ethnic groups in each successively younger cohort. However, the relative advantage of whites is about the same for all three cohorts. In Cohort C, who were 55 to 64 in 1980, the median education for whites is slightly higher than high-school graduation, while that for African American women (the next highest group) is only 9.6 years.

Occupation

At ages 55 to 64, minority men in these cohorts are heavily concentrated in semiskilled and unskilled blue-collar jobs, while white men are about equally likely to hold semi- or unskilled blue-collar, skilled blue-collar, or professional/managerial jobs. Hispanic women are also disproportionately likely to hold semi- or unskilled blue-collar jobs. African American women are most likely to be found in service jobs, and white women in clerical ones.

Minority-group members in the younger cohorts are not quite so heavily concentrated in one occupational category as their counterparts in the oldest cohort, but the basic pattern of distribution is similar. There has been *some* growth in the number of minority members in the higher-status occupations. However, the most marked change, reflecting a restructuring of the labor market, has been for minority women. Both Hispanic and African American women who were 55 to 64 in 1980 were more likely than ever before to be in non–household service. The increase for African American women has been at the expense of the household service category. For Hispanic women the largest corresponding decline was in semi- and unskilled blue collar work, though this remains the largest single category of occupation for Hispanic women.

Employment History

Whites are more likely to be have worked 50 weeks or more in the past year than minority group members of the same sex at ages 55 to 64. Men in the younger cohorts are more likely than those in the older cohorts to have been out of the labor force for the entire preceding year in those ages, while women in the younger cohorts are less likely to have been out of the labor force. Ethnic differences in the percentages who did not work do not vary much among the three cohorts, though the number of Hispanic women in the work force is strikingly larger for the younger cohorts. (Nevertheless they remain less likely to work than white or African American women.) On the other hand, the number who did work but experienced long periods of layoff or unemployment, is smaller for minorities in the younger cohorts than it has been for those in the older cohorts.

This greater stability may be due to the rise of employment in the service sector and, to a somewhat smaller degree, the clerical field. Although jobs in these areas may pay no better (or even worse) than unskilled labor in construction or manufacturing, they are less seasonal in their nature.

There is no consistent pattern of differences between whites, African Americans, and Hispanics in the likelihood of holding part- or full-time jobs.

Place of Residence

Both African Americans and Hispanics in these cohorts are more likely than whites to live in the South, where pay is lower than in the nation as a whole. The differences between African Americans and whites are smaller with each successive cohort, because whites in younger cohorts are more likely than those in older cohorts to live in the South, and African Americans in younger cohorts are more likely than those in older cohorts to live outside the South.

The geographic concentration of Hispanics is not regional, but localized within a few states. (Thus, those of Mexican descent are found largely in Texas and California, Cubans are concentrated in Florida, and Puerto Ricans in New York.) However, in the 1990s there has been greater dispersion of the Hispanic population. There does not seem to be much variation in Hispanic income among the states with largest Hispanic populations.

Size of place as well as region has an influence on income. Despite the conventional image of the central city as the heart of minority poverty, central-city residence had a slight positive influence on family income at this age, with other variables controlled, though this is significant only for Cohort A. Significant at all ages is the disadvantage of living in a rural area.

Sex and Marital Status

Married couples fare better economically than singles. Although men have higher earnings and higher occupational status than women, unmarried women fare better than unmarried men. This is probably a reflection of widows' pension benefits, because for these cohorts women in the age group 55 to 64 were much more likely to be widowed than divorced. On the other hand, unmarried men in this age/cohort group are slightly more likely to be divorced than widowed.

Whites are more likely to be married at ages 55 to 64 than Hispanics or African Americans. Whites have the lowest percentages of both widowhood and separation or divorce, and African Americans have the highest. This is true for both sexes, though women of all three ethnic groups are more likely to be unmarried than are men. Among the three cohorts, women in the youngest suffer the least marital disruption and women in the oldest the most, regardless of ethnicity. Across ethnicities, widowhood at ages 55 to 64 has declined from cohort to cohort. Divorce and separation has also increased consistently, but at a slower rate, so that there is a net increase in the number still married.

Contribution of Ethnicity to Family Income and Poverty

With sex, age (within the age group), place of residence (both region and size of place), education, occupation, labor history (hours per week and weeks per year), marital status, and headship status controlled, African American ethnicity subtracted about $5,000 in 1990 dollars from family income at ages 55 to 64. Hispanic ethnicity did not contribute significantly to income when these variables were controlled. However, these variables may be the vehicles of discrimination and are certainly barriers to economic achievement for Hispanics as well as for African Americans.

There is some sign of the declining influence of race over time, in that the regression coefficient, expressed in 1990 dollars, is smaller for the younger cohorts: –$5,513 for Cohort A, –$4,760 for Cohort B, and –$4,440 for Cohort C.

With the same variables controlled, both African American and Hispanic ethnicity reduced the ratio of family income to the poverty level. That is, both minorities still faced increased likelihood of poverty even with occupation, education, and other sociodemographic variables controlled. The effect was larger for African Americans than Hispanics, but significant at the .001 level for both. Further, though Hispanic ethnicity had a smaller effect in Cohort C than in Cohort B, African American ethnicity had about the same effect in both cohorts. These findings suggest that small gains in ethnic equality of income in the study cohorts may not have extended to those with the lowest incomes who still suffer a penalty based on their ethnic status.

The Second Question

2. *How did the income differences among ethnic groups change as these cohorts aged? Are any of the meanings of double jeopardy supported by these differences? Did the variables that helped explain ethnic differences when the cohorts were younger gain, lose, or maintain their explanatory power as the cohorts aged?*

To answer this question requires comparison within cohorts over the course of aging, rather than the comparison across cohorts at the same age implied in the preceding question This topic was addressed in Chapter 4.

Ethnic Changes in Income as Cohorts Age

Income declined sharply from ages 55 to 64 to 65 to 74 for all three ethnic groups in each of the cohorts. Whites and African Americans (with one exception in the periods studied) showed additional but smaller income losses in the decades following initial retirement. Hispanics showed a similar pattern in 1960 to 1980. In 1990, all cohorts of Hispanics showed income gains, which may represent a more accurate estimate due to a larger sample rather than a meaningful change in income for this group.

Where income losses were found for all three ethnic groups, they were proportionately larger among whites. For example, in Cohort A, median family income for whites fell 32.4 percent from ages 55 to 64 to ages 65 to 74, while African American income fell only 23.8 percent. As a result, the ratio of African American to white income for that cohort rose from .490 at ages 55 to 64 to .553. Additional declines brought the ratio to .608 for 75 to 84 year olds and .702 for those 85 and older in that cohort. The same pattern is seen between Hispanic and white income for that cohort. There is more fluctuation in relative income among ethnic groups in Cohorts B and C than in A, but the general trend remains toward leveling.

The percent in poverty can only be observed before and after age 65 for Cohorts B and C, and findings from those two cohorts are diametrically opposite. In Cohort B, both Hispanics and African Americans experience higher percentages in poverty relative to whites in the postretirement years than in the years preceding retirement. In 1970, when people in Cohort B were 55 to 64 years old, Hispanics were 1.7 times as likely and African Americans 2.5 times as likely as whites to be in poverty. In 1980, when these people were 65 to 74, Hispanics were 2.2 times as likely and African Americans 3.2 times as likely to be in poverty. Thus, Cohort B exhibited double jeopardy of falling into poverty.

In Cohort C, by contrast, Hispanics went from 2.6 times to 2.3 times as likely as whites to be in poverty and African Americans went from 3.8 times to 3.5 times as that cohort aged from 55 to 64 to ages 65 to 74. For Cohort C, then, the leveling trend seen in income was also seen for poverty.

Younger cohorts fared better than older ones when comparisons for the same age and ethnic group were made, but the *differences among ethnic groups* in poverty were larger for the younger cohorts.

Is the Double Jeopardy Hypothesis Supported?

Neither double jeopardy (interactive effect of age and ethnicity) nor parallel jeopardy (additive independent effects of age and ethnicity) applies to the family income of African Americans and Hispanics, relative to whites in today's oldest cohorts. Though they are economically disadvantaged relative to whites, older African Americans and Hispanics have incomes closer to that of their white age-mates than they did when they were in late middle age. Furthermore, the independent effects of being African American, with relevant sociodemographic variables controlled, decline in later years, with some fluctuations. (There is no significant effect of Hispanic ethnicity when these other variables are controlled.) Thus, the leveling hypothesis is supported. The apparent explanation for this is the dependence of most older Americans on incomes stemming from their past employment—pensions and Social Security. Since the range in these payments is smaller than the range in salaries, the degree of inequality is reduced.

The jeopardy of poverty is supported in one cohort, while a leveling effect is seen in data for another. Study of a larger number of cohorts may be necessary to see whether this represents true cohort differences, some unidentified historical influence, or just some "noise" in the data.

Explanatory Variables

Very broadly speaking, the variables that explained income differences at ages 55 to 64 remained significant, but they had smaller constant-dollar impacts on income differences at older ages. This was true for all three cohorts.

In Cohort A, only *African American*, *married*, *education*, and *weeks worked*, declined significantly from ages 55 to 64 to ages 65 to 74. *Hours worked* became more important over this age change. However when Cohort A aged from 65 to 74 to 75 to 84, and when Cohort B aged from 55 to 64 to 65 to 74, most of the control variables had significant but weaker influence.

Some changes in significance may reflect period as well as aging effects. The declining impact of southern residence and the reversal of the effect of central-city residence (from positive in 1960 to negative in 1990) appear to follow the calendar rather than the age of the respondents. At the same time, the effect of these variables is mitigated by age, in that older people on Federal retirement funds and, to a smaller degree, pensions from large corporations, receive incomes that do not vary with place of residence.

The Third Question

3. *How do assets such as savings and investments contribute to inequality among ethnic groups? What is the role of political policies and government programs in perpetuating or reducing inequity? What are ethnic differences in the resource available from family assistance and living arrangements?*

Chapter 5 surveys the wide field of other resources to provide some tentative answers to these questions.

Home Ownership

For every cohort/age combination, whites were more likely than African Americans or Hispanics to own their home. There is leveling in the differences between African Americans and whites in terms of this variable. Cohort A sees leveling because institutionalized whites were more likely than institutionalized minority group members to be former home owners. In the younger cohorts, African Americans show larger *gains* in home ownership relative to whites. Both processes lead to leveling. Hispanics show fluctuation, relative to whites, but no clear pattern of either leveling or double jeopardy. Within ethnic groups, younger cohorts are more likely to own their own homes than older ones.

Income from Wealth

In period data for the three cohorts in 1980 only, whites are much more likely to have income from interest, dividends, and rent than African Americans or Hispanics. Among those who have such income, whites, on average, have higher incomes (reflecting larger assets) than members of either minority group. For example, over 70 percent of whites in Cohort A had income from interest, and among those who did, the median annual interest was $524 in 1980. For that same time and cohort, less than 22 percent of African Americans had any income from interest, and among those who did, the median was only $100.

Income from assets is a proxy measure of reserve capital with which to meet the emergencies that become more common in old age. Therefore this ethnic difference is not only larger than most of the others measured in this study, but it also has more critical implications for well-being. Although the number of older whites with substantial income from assets is relatively small, this difference suggests that the leveling seen in family income may overstate the approach to financial equality among older adults.

Political Policies and Government Programs

In data limited to 1980, whites 65 and older are more likely to have pensions and other non–need-based income sources than African Americans and Hispanics. This includes OASDI. Minority-group members are more likely to receive food stamps, subsidized rent, and other need-based payments, as expected from their much greater likelihood of poverty. However, the value of the need-based assistance is much smaller than the value of the non–need-based assistance. For example, combined non-need-based government payments (including Social Security and government pensions, but not including veterans' benefits) averaged \$3,120 for whites 65 to 74 in 1980, and \$2,386 for African Americans. Supplemental Security Income (SSI) averaged \$870 per year for whites and \$1,111 for African Americans that age, while food stamp values were \$330 for whites and \$408 for African Americans.

For each ethnic group, the proportion receiving pensions is greater for the young elderly than the old elderly, but the cohort-specific ethnic differences are very similar. Despite the inequities in the distribution of Social Security, it is the major source of leveling. It works to level income, because a large majority of all ethnic groups receive their major income from this source, and the variation between the highest and lowest payments is smaller than salary differences.

Living Arrangements and Family Assistance

These data do not give us a clear picture of financial support from families, which is usually informal, unmeasured, and irregular. In 1980, less than 1 percent reported income from regular contributions of family or others in all ethnic groups and all cohorts.

Aside from such regular contributions, the most clearly observable contribution is in living arrangements—the relatives who take an older family member to live with them. However, this type of family assistance, while preferable to institutionalization, is usually not the ideal living arrangement of either older or younger family members. Therefore it is difficult to evaluate the positive contribution of such an arrangement.

Although most older people of all ethnicities do live as the head of a household or spouse of the head, whites are the most likely to do so at every age. When compared at the same age, younger cohorts are the most likely to live as head or spouse, but ethnic differences are not smaller in these cohorts. Hispanics who do not live as head or spouse are more likely than whites or African Americans to live with family members. This is especially true of Hispanic women.

While there are ethnic differences in the likelihood that an older person will live independently, there are not significant ethnic differences in the likelihood that younger people (35 to 44 and 45 to 54) will have someone over 65 living with them. The small but consistent demographic predictors of sharing living quarters with an older person are a marital status other than currently married with spouse present, high income, and a low ratio of people younger than 65 to the number of bedrooms.

The Fourth Question

4. *What do the findings of this research, in light of the current trends among younger African Americans and Hispanics, suggest about the future of minority elders in the United States?*

This study has dealt with three historical cohorts of elderly—those who were 65 to 74, 75 to 84, and 85 and older in 1990. They were educated and began their careers before the major civil-rights legislation of this century. It is not unexpected to see large income differences among whites, African Americans, and Hispanics of these cohorts, in both middle and old age. But what of younger whites and minority group members? What can they expect as they grow older?

The answer can only be speculative, but the earlier chapters of this work provide some clues. For all preretirement age groups in these cohorts (Cohort A in 1960; Cohort B in 1960 and 1970; and Cohort C in 1960, 1970, and 1980), the two most important predictors of family income (i.e. those with the largest standardized regression coefficients) were *education* and *marital status*. Therefore, a quick look at education, marital status, and family income of the younger cohorts should provide grounds for some informed guesses.

Education of the Younger Cohorts

Tables 6-1 through 6-3 below, drawn from published census and Current Population Report data, show education by sex as measured by the percent who have at least a high school diploma in each decade from 1970 to 1990. They demonstrate a continuation of the trend seen in the three elder cohorts. With few exceptions, within ethnic groups each younger cohort is more likely to have graduated from high school than the one preceding it.

There is also a clear narrowing of differences between African Americans and whites with successive cohorts. In Cohort N, born 1966 to 1970, (20 to 24 in 1990), African American men were almost 94 percent as likely to have graduated from high school as white men. By contrast, in Cohort J, born 1946 to 1950, (20 to 24 in 1970) African American men are only 73 percent as likely as white men to have completed high school.

The trend is the same for African American women, and for Hispanic women at most ages. Hispanic men show a less consistent pattern. They appear to be losing ground, if one compares cohorts at ages younger than 30 or 50 to 54. For the age groups from 30 to 49, 1990 saw the highest education level relative to whites, but rates in 1980 data are lower than those in 1970 data. At all ages, Hispanics in 1980 and 1990 are still substantially less likely to have completed high school than their white and African American counterparts.

When cohorts rather than age groups are examined, the proportion who graduated from high school increases over each ten-year period for African Americans and whites, though the magnitude of the increase is larger for African Americans. The proportions of this increase accounted for by continuing education, systematic mortality differences, and exaggeration of educational attainment cannot be assessed from these data.

There are programs to help young African Americans who drop out of school to finish their education. There are also higher age-specific mortality rates among those young African Americans who are least likely to have finished high school. However, some of the increases shown in table 6-1 appear too good to be true. For example, in 1970, 59 percent of African American men ages 20 to 24 had completed high school. Data for the same cohort twenty years later show that 79.4 percent of African American men ages 40 to 44 had done so.

Table 6-1. Percent Who Have Graduated from High School, by Age, Sex, Ethnicity,[a] and Year

	1970			*1980*			*1990/91*[b]		
Age	*W*	*H*	*AA*	*W*	*H*	*AA*	*W*	*H*	*AA*
MEN									
20 to 24	80.7	58.2	59.0	83.6	58.4	69.8	84.2	54.9	78.8
25 to 29	76.3	53.2	54.7	87.0	58.4	73.8	85.1	56.4	83.5
30 to 34	71.4	47.2	46.8	86.9	56.3	72.4	87.0	57.6	83.2
35 to 39	67.0	42.6	40.0	82.0	49.6	64.4	88.0	57.7	82.3
40 to 44	60.0	36.5	31.8	77.3	44.8	56.0	88.2	56.2	79.4
45 to 49	58.3	34.5	27.3	72.7	40.9	47.9	85.1	51.7	70.6
50 to 54	52.4	32.3	21.8	64.9	35.5	37.8	79.8	43.3	57.1
WOMEN									
20 to 24	80.9	57.5	64.1	85.9	61.8	76.7	86.3	62.3	79.4
25 to 29	71.8	48.7	56.0	87.2	59.2	76.5	86.6	57.1	80.1
30 to 34	71.3	42.3	48.8	85.9	54.4	73.4	88.1	60.2	81.2
35 to 39	67.6	37.0	42.6	81.5	47.6	65.6	89.9	59.7	81.3
40 to 44	63.9	33.3	36.1	77.0	43.1	58.0	88.6	56.3	79.9
45 to 49	61.5	31.8	30.0	72.6	37.7	50.4	85.1	48.9	71.9
50 to 54	54.9	27.6	23.9	67.8	33.0	41.5	81.7	48.3	62.5

Sources: U.S. Bureau of the Census, 1973b, 1984, 1992d.

[a]For this and all tables, ethnic groups are represented by W=white, H=Hispanic, and AA=African American.

[b]These data had not been published for the 1990 census at the time this book went to press. Therefore, Current Population Survey data were used for this time.

Table 6-2. Ratio of Percent African Americans to Percent Whites Graduating from High School, by Sex, Age, and Cohort

	1970		*1980*		*1990*	
Age	*Cohort*	*Ratio*	*Cohort*	*Ratio*	*Cohort*	*Ratio*
MEN						
20–24	J	.731	L	.835	N	.936
25–29	I	.718	K	.848	M	.981
30–34	H	.656	J	.833	L	.956
35–39	G	.598	I	.785	K	.935
40–44	F	.531	H	.724	J	.900
45–49	E	.469	G	.659	I	.830
50–54	D	.416	F	.582	H	.716
WOMEN						
20–24	J	.793	L	.893	N	.920
25–29	I	.780	K	.877	M	.925
30–34	H	.685	J	.854	L	.922
35–39	G	.630	I	.805	K	.904
40–44	F	.565	H	.753	J	.902
45–49	E	.487	G	.694	I	.845
50–54	D	.435	F	.612	H	.765

Source: Computed from table 6-1.

Table 6-3. Ratio of Percent Hispanics to Percent Whites Graduating from High School, by Sex, Age, and Cohort

	1970		*1980*		*1990*	
Age	*Cohort*	*Ratio*	*Cohort*	*Ratio*	*Cohort*	*Ratio*
MEN						
20–24	J	.721	L	.699	N	.652
25–29	I	.697	K	.671	M	.663
30–34	H	.660	J	.648	L	.662
35–39	G	.636	I	.605	K	.656
40–44	F	.609	H	.580	J	.637
45–49	E	.592	G	.563	I	.608
50–54	D	.616	F	.547	H	.543

Table 6-3 is continued on the next page.

Table 6-3. Ratio of Percent Hispanics to Percent Whites Graduating from High School, by Sex, Age, and Cohort (continued)

	1970		1980		1990	
Age	*Cohort*	*Ratio*	*Cohort*	*Ratio*	*Cohort*	*Ratio*
WOMEN						
20–24	J	.711	L	.719	N	.722
25–29	I	.679	K	.679	M	.659
30–34	H	.593	J	.633	L	.683
35–39	G	.547	I	.584	K	.664
40–44	F	.521	H	.559	J	.635
45–49	E	.516	G	.519	I	.575
50–54	D	.503	F	.487	H	.591

Source: Computed from table 6-1.

The pattern for Hispanics is quite different. For all cohorts of Hispanic men and more than half of the cohorts of Hispanic women represented here, there was some *decline* in the proportion who had earned a high school diploma. Most of the differences are fairly small and may be due to small fluctuations in the sample. However additions of less-educated immigrants to the population over the 10-year intervals may also have played a role.

The proportion of minority group members completing four or more years of college remains quite small relative to whites, especially among men. For Cohort K (25 to 29 in 1980), over a quarter of white men had completed at least four years of college in 1980, and about 28 percent by 1990. This compares to 17 percent of African American men and 11 percent of Hispanic men in the same cohort. The difference between white and African American women is slightly smaller, because white women were less likely and African American women somewhat more likely than their male counterparts to complete college. Hispanic women were similar to Hispanic men in this cohort, around 11 percent by 1990.

Younger cohorts show less ethnic equality in college completion than Cohort K. However, the experience of Cohort K suggests that African American and Hispanic students complete their college education more slowly (consistent with a greater likelihood of working their way through college). Therefore, younger cohorts may appear more unequal while members are still in their twenties than they will be when members reach their late thirties.

From the perspective of education, then, the future of tomorrow's minority elderly shows a mingled pattern of hope and frustration. There has been continuous improvement from cohort to cohort, and the gap in high school graduates has closed substantially between whites and African Americans (though not between whites and Hispanics). Yet, just as this benchmark of education is being reached by African Americans, the normative goal is changing. A college degree rather than a high school diploma is increasingly the minimum requirement for good jobs for these cohorts, and here both African Americans and Hispanics continue to lag behind.

Marital Status in the Younger Cohorts

In 1980 and 1990, whites of every age-sex group were more likely than Hispanics (except those ages 20 to 24), and Hispanics more likely than African Americans, to be married with spouse present, the best status for achieving high family income (see table 6-4). Comparison of age groups in the two time periods show opposite trends for the two ethnic minorities. Hispanics in 1990 were more like whites in their marital status than Hispanics the same age a decade before, suggesting a reduction in this source of income inequality. However, African Americans were less like whites in 1990 than in 1980 (except for men ages 20 to 24), adding to this source of inequality for African Americans.

People of every ethnic-sex-age combination were more likely to be married in 1980 than in 1990. Hence the narrowing of inequality among Hispanics was due to slower declines than experienced by whites, while African Americans experienced even greater declines than whites.

For example, in 1980 almost 76 percent of white women ages 30 to 34 were married. Just under 46 percent of African American women in that age group were married—60 percent as many as white women. In 1990 only 70 percent of white women in this age group were married, but the rate for African American women had dropped to 38 percent—54 percent as many as white women.

Table 6-4. Percent Now Married with Spouse Present, by Sex, Ethnicity,[a] and Age for Those Aged 20 to 54, and Ratio of Minority to White Population of That Marital Status

	Percent			*Ratio*	
Age	*W*	*H*	*AA*	*AA/W*	*H/W*
			1980		
MEN					
20 to 24	27.9	29.9	15.3	0.548	1.072
25 to 29	59.1	57.3	40.5	0.685	0.970
30 to 34	74.2	69.9	54.3	0.732	0.942
35 to 44	81.5	75.2	61.9	0.760	0.922
45 to 54	84.0	77.6	63.9	0.762	0.924
WOMEN					
20 to 24	43.1	43.8	21.6	0.501	1.016
25 to 29	67.4	62.4	38.9	0.577	0.926
30 to 34	75.9	68.2	45.8	0.603	0.899
35 to 44	79.1	69.8	49.4	0.625	0.882
45 to 54	78.1	66.7	49.7	0.637	0.853
			1990		
MEN					
20 to 24	19.5	23.4	12.3	0.633	1.200
25 to 29	48.6	48.2	30.5	0.627	0.992
30 to 34	64.5	61.7	42.1	0.653	0.957
35 to 44	73.3	69.9	52.2	0.712	0.954
45 to 54	79.2	74.9	59.4	0.750	0.946
WOMEN					
20 to 24	32.1	37.4	15.7	0.489	1.165
25 to 29	60.1	56.7	30.7	0.511	0.943
30 to 34	70.0	63.2	37.9	0.541	0.903
35 to 44	72.8	64.9	42.4	0.583	0.891
45 to 54	73.7	63.9	44.9	0.610	0.867

Source: U.S. Bureau of the Census, 1984, table 264; 1992a.

[a]For this and all tables, ethnic groups are represented by W=white, H=Hispanic, and AA=African American.

Tables 6-5 and 6-6 show the percent whose current marital status is widowed or divorced, respectively. Although the number of widows and widowers in these younger cohorts is relatively small, African

been in 1980. With some exceptions, the reduction in widowhood has been proportionately greater for African Americans and Hispanics, resulting in greater equality in this risk factor over time.

The numbers of men and women whose current status is divorced are much larger than the numbers of widows in the younger cohorts, and the pattern of ethnic differences is more complex. In general, Hispanics are less likely than whites to be divorced. In 1980, three groups of Hispanics had a higher proportion of divorcees than whites (men ages 45 to 54 and women 35 to 44 and 45 to 54). These middle-aged Hispanics mirror the experience of the study cohorts, being more likely than African Americans and less likely than whites to be divorced.

African Americans are less likely than whites to be divorced in ages less than 30, and slightly more likely to be divorced in ages older than 30. Divorce statistics, however, understate African American marital disruption, because African Americans are more likely than whites to separate without going through the formality of divorce (Cherlin, 1981).

If we look at the proportion divorced or separated combined (table 6-7), African Americans (except at the youngest ages, when they are less likely to have ever married) and Hispanic women, are more likely than whites to experience disruption. Hispanic men are less likely than whites to be divorced or separated in the age groups younger than 35.

The trend over time is toward greater equality. All groups have disruption rates closer to whites in 1990 than in 1980. If we compare data within cohorts for those that appear at both data points, (those 20 to 24, 25 to 29, and 30 to 34 in 1980), the picture is a bit more mixed. The trend for Hispanics of both genders and African American men is toward greater equality, but African American women show less equality as the cohorts age in two of the three cohorts.

Income Patterns in the Younger Cohorts

Income in these young cohorts is both a predictor of future income and a resource for old age (because it represents the ability to buy a home, invest, or save). Table 6-8 shows median personal income by age, sex, and ethnicity for these cohorts in 1969, 1979, and 1990. As that table shows, changes over time have not been consistent for all age-gender-ethnic groups.

Table 6-5. Percent Currently Widowed, by Sex, Ethnicity,[a] and Age, for Those Aged 20 to 54, and Ratio of Minority to White Population of that Marital Status

	Percent			*Ratio*	
Age	*W*	*H*	*AA*	*AA/W*	*H/W*
			1980		
MEN					
20 to 24	—	0.1	0.1	—	—
25 to 29	0.1	0.2	0.3	3.000	2.000
30 to 34	0.2	0.2	0.5	2.500	1.000
35 to 44	0.3	0.5	1.2	3.596	1.601
45 to 54	1.2	1.4	3.6	3.136	1.253
WOMEN					
20 to 24	0.2	0.3	0.3	1.500	1.500
25 to 29	0.4	0.7	1.1	2.750	1.750
30 to 34	0.7	1.3	2.3	3.286	1.857
35 to 44	1.7	2.6	5.1	3.010	1.504
45 to 54	6.1	7.2	13.6	2.240	1.185
			1990		
MEN					
20 to 24	0.1	0.1	0.1	1.000	1.000
25 to 29	0.1	0.2	0.2	2.000	2.000
30 to 34	0.2	0.3	0.3	1.500	1.500
35 to 44	0.3	0.5	0.8	2.827	1.667
45 to 54	0.9	1.3	2.5	2.806	1.444
WOMEN					
20 to 24	0.2	0.3	0.3	1.500	1.500
25 to 29	0.4	0.6	0.5	1.367	1.500
30 to 34	0.6	1.1	1.2	1.965	1.833
35 to 44	1.3	2.3	3.3	2.520	1.769
45 to 54	4.4	6.1	10.1	2.288	1.386

Source: U.S. Bureau of the Census., 1984, table 264; 1992a.

[a]For this and all tables, ethnic groups are represented by W=white, H=Hispanic, and AA=African American.

Table 6-6. Percent Currently Divorced, by Sex, Ethnicity,[a] and Age, for Those Aged 20 to 54, and Ratio of Minority to White Population of that Marital Status

	Percent			*Ratio*	
Age	*W*	*H*	*AA*	*AA/W*	*H/W*
			1980		
MEN					
20 to 24	2.4	2.0	1.2	0.500	0.833
25 to 29	6.9	5.6	6.0	0.870	0.812
30 to 34	8.6	7.2	10.2	1.186	0.837
35 to 44	8.1	7.1	11.3	1.400	0.878
45 to 54	6.7	6.9	10.9	1.618	1.024
WOMEN					
20 to 24	4.5	3.7	2.8	0.622	0.822
25 to 29	9.1	8.1	10.0	1.099	0.890
30 to 34	10.8	10.3	15.3	1.417	0.954
35 to 44	10.8	11.1	16.5	1.525	1.026
45 to 54	8.9	11.1	14.2	1.591	1.247
			1990		
MEN					
20 to 24	1.7	1.2	0.9	0.538	0.706
25 to 29	6.0	4.3	4.1	0.688	0.717
30 to 34	9.5	7.3	8.3	0.872	0.768
35 to 44	12.2	10.4	14.4	1.182	0.852
45 to 54	11.9	10.8	16.1	1.356	0.908
WOMEN					
20 to 24	3.5	2.6	1.8	0.501	0.743
25 to 29	8.6	6.9	6.4	0.740	0.802
30 to 34	11.6	10.5	12.3	1.063	0.905
35 to 44	15.0	14.2	20.3	1.353	0.947
45 to 54	15.2	15.3	21.4	1.406	1.007

Source: U.S. Bureau of the Census, 1984, table 264; 1992a.

[a]For this and all tables, ethnic groups are represented by W=white, H=Hispanic, and AA=African American.

Table 6-7. Ratio of African American to White and Hispanic to White of Proportion Divorced or Separated

	Ratios			
	1980		*1990*	
Age	*AA/W*	*H/W*	*AA/W*	*H/W*
MEN				
20 to 24	1.333	1.608	0.919	0.963
25 to 29	1.602	1.340	1.071	0.911
30 to 34	1.874	1.303	1.273	0.949
35 to 44	2.107	1.396	1.584	1.021
45 to 54	2.423	1.549	1.809	1.101
WOMEN				
20 to 24	1.309	1.383	0.882	1.073
25 to 29	1.777	1.292	1.183	1.070
30 to 34	2.126	1.343	1.547	1.166
35 to 44	2.320	1.426	1.802	1.203
45 to 54	2.481	1.705	1.893	1.283

Source: Calculated from table 6-6.

[a]For this and all tables, ethnic groups are represented by W=white, H=Hispanic, and AA=African American.

White men in ages 40 to 44 and all younger ages have seen a decline in constant-dollar income over the twenty-year interval presented here. African American men in the youngest ages (25 to 29 and 30 to 34) and Hispanic men at all ages have also seen a decline over this period. By contrast, white men at ages 45 and older and African American men at ages 40 and older have seen an increase in constant dollar income.

Women have, in general, seen more increase in income than men of their age and ethnic group, though their incomes remain much smaller. White women at every age and Hispanic and African American women ages 35 and older have higher incomes in 1990 than women in the same age-ethnic group in 1970 or 1980, though older Hispanics and whites saw a decline from 1970 to 1980 before the rise.

Table 6-8. Median Income in 1990 Dollars by Age, Sex, and Ethnicity[a]

	1969			1979			1990		
Age	*W*	*H*	*AA*	*W*	*H*	*AA*	*W*	*H*	*AA*
MEN									
25 to 29	$25,841	$20,754	$18,271	$20,901	$16,027	$14,674	$20,153	$13,641	$14,333
30 to 34	29,856	23,082	19,683	26,271	19,182	18,202	25,248	16,731	15,858
35 to 39	31,661	23,739	19,959	30,530	20,728	19,978	29,803	17,993	19,352
40 to 44	32,173	23,957	19,568	31,760	20,843	20,102	31,615	18,898	21,218
45 to 49	31,641	23,331	18,777	32,030	20,786	19,483	32,217	18,245	20,656
50 to 54	29,748	22,074	17,284	30,628	19,953	17,661	31,235	17,557	19,829
WOMEN									
25 to 29	11,763	10,008	10,557	12,231	9,773	10,545	13,659	9,413	8,980
30 to 34	10,611	10,086	10,652	11,830	9,892	12,146	12,949	8,618	11,225
35 to 39	11,076	10,298	10,557	11,733	9,990	12,133	14,026	11,013	14,257
40 to 44	12,026	10,476	9,921	11,968	10,082	11,489	14,963	10,548	15,505
45 to 49	12,690	10,200	9,028	11,958	9,709	10,523	14,940	10,781	14,282
50 to 54	12,720	9,533	7,738	9,758	9,062	9,049	13,356	9,085	12,425

Sources: U.S. Bureau of the Census, 1973b, 1984, 1991.

[a]For this and all tables, ethnic groups are represented by W=white, H=Hispanic, and AA=African American.

How does income equality change as a result of these separate ethnic, age, and gender patterns? Tables 6-9 and 6-10 present ratios of African American to white and Hispanic to white income, respectively. Like tables 6-2 and 6-3, they may be read across rows to compare people of a given age at two points of time (e.g., those 25 to 29 in 1970 with those 25 to 29 in 1980 and 1990). They may also be compared by cohort letter to see changes within a cohort at two points in time (e.g., those in Cohort I who were 25 to 29 in 1970, 35 to 39 in 1980, and 45 to 49 in 1990).

Although different measures of income are used, the ratio of African American to white income for men is better for younger cohorts when comparisons are made across the same age group. This is consistent with the improvements from Cohorts A to C in preretirement ages demonstrated in Chapter 4. The two age groups between ages 30 and 39 were the exception. The cohorts in those age groups in 1980 saw more equal income than either the ones that went before or the ones that came after. Women echo this pattern, except at the youngest age group, where the 1970 cohort had the advantage. Women also differ in that African American women had higher median personal incomes than white women for five of the 18 age groups (represented by ratios greater than 1), while white men had higher personal income than African American men at every age.

Although comparison of younger and older cohorts at the same age reflects reduction of income differences among African Americans and whites, examination of cohorts across the ten-year span is less encouraging. In every cohort of men for which there are two or more observations (Cohorts F through K), and for three cohorts of women (F through H), the ratio declined over time, demonstrating less income equality as the cohort aged. For example, African American men in Cohort I had incomes almost 71 percent those of white men in Cohort I at ages 25 to 29, but only 65 percent the incomes of whites at ages 35 to 39 and 64 percent at ages 45 to 49. These data cannot prove, but strongly suggest, that opportunities for African Americans may be increasing for opening-level positions to a much greater degree than opportunities for later career advancement. The increases seen in the younger cohorts of women may be related to later timing in the completion of education and the beginning of a real career as suggested in the educational findings above.

Table 6-9. Ratios of African American to White Median Income by Sex and Age

Age	*1969* Cohort	*1969* Ratio	*1979* Cohort	*1979* Ratio	*1990*[a] Cohort	*1990*[a] Ratio
MEN						
25 to 29	I	0.707	K	.702	M	0.711
30 to 34	H	0.659	J	.693	L	0.628
35 to 39	G	0.630	I	.654	K	0.649
40 to 44	F	0.608	H	.633	J	0.671
45 to 49	E	0.593	G	.608	I	0.641
50 to 54	D	0.591	F	.577	H	0.635
WOMEN						
25 to 29	I	0.897	K	.862	M	0.657
30 to 34	H	1.004	J	1.027	L	0.867
35 to 39	G	0.953	I	1.071	K	1.016
40 to 44	F	0.824	H	.979	J	1.036
45 to 49	E	0.711	G	.878	I	0.956
50 to 54	D	0.608	F	.757	H	0.930

Source: Computed from table 6-8.
[a]Past year's income reported on 1970 and 1980 Census and 1991 *Current Population Reports*.

Following the pattern seen in Cohorts A through C throughout this research, Hispanic men in the younger cohorts had incomes between those of whites and African Americans in 1969 and 1979. In 1990, the finding is very different for these younger cohorts. The older adults in the study cohorts saw an increase of Hispanic income, even exceeding that of whites for some observations. By contrast, the Hispanics in the younger cohorts had the lowest incomes of the three groups.

The trend for Hispanics over time is less encouraging than for African Americans. Both men and women of this ethnic group fare worse, relative to whites their own age at the previous observation point or points. Further, like African Americans, Hispanic cohorts experience less equality with whites as they age. For example, Hispanic men ages 25 to 29 in 1969 had a median income 80 percent that of whites, but for the same cohort in 1979 the median was less than 70 percent of whites; in 1990 it was only 56 percent.

Extrapolating from findings in the older cohorts that there is no significant, independent contribution of Hispanic ethnicity to income, and taking into consideration the lower educational levels of the younger Hispanic cohorts, it seems likely that this lower income is due to the disproportionate presence of migrants (and perhaps second-generation barrio dwellers) in the younger age groups.

Table 6-10. Ratios of Hispanic to White Median Income by Sex and Age

	1969		*1979*		*1990*[a]	
Age	*Cohort*	*Ratio*	*Cohort*	*Ratio*	*Cohort*	*Ratio*
MEN						
25 to 29	I	.803	K	.767	M	.677
30 to 34	H	.773	J	.730	L	.663
35 to 39	G	.749	I	.679	K	.604
40 to 44	F	.745	H	.656	J	.598
45 to 49	E	.737	G	.649	I	.566
50 to 54	D	.742	F	.651	H	.562
WOMEN						
25 to 29	I	.851	K	.799	M	.689
30 to 34	H	.950	J	.836	L	.666
35 to 39	G	.930	I	.885	K	.785
40 to 44	F	.871	H	.851	J	.705
45 to 49	E	.804	G	.842	I	.722
50 to 54	D	.749	F	.788	H	.680

Source: Computed from table 6-8.
[a]Past year's income reported on 1970 and 1980 Census and 1991 *Current Population Reports*.

Theoretical Issues Revisited

As stated in Chapter 1, it is not possible to test directly the operation of competing hierarchies. Instances where data or historical information are consistent with these ideas can be pointed out, but only the relationship among variables, not that among systems, can be empirically tested within the framework of this research. In this summary chapter, it is appropriate to return to the theoretical system of hierarchies identified by Lenski and reflect on these data in light of this theoretical framework.

chies identified by Lenski and reflect on these data in light of this theoretical framework.

The Racial/Ethnic Hierarchy

This study examined the United States's largest racial minority (African Americans) and a primarily white ethnic group (Hispanics, specifically excluding people who are racially African American and culturally or linguistically Hispanic). Comparisons of each of these groups with whites suggests that race and cultural ethnicity are perhaps two hierarchies rather than a single one. In the three cohorts of African Americans studied, their ethnic status was significantly correlated with income when other sociodemographic variables were controlled. In those same cohorts, Hispanic ethnicity was not significantly correlated with income, though it was significantly correlated with poverty. Further, at every age, older Hispanics have higher average incomes than African Americans. This is true even when the lowest income quartiles are examined. Dropping average incomes (relative to whites) in younger cohorts parallels dropping average educational levels (again relative to whites). This appears to be due to immigration or the effects of prior high fertility in the poorest Hispanic communities.

Although this is far from conclusive, given the small and somewhat problematic nature of the Hispanic sample, these data suggest that the problems of Hispanics in the United States today are largely those of any immigrant population. Those who have been assimilated into the majority culture, or who can appear to have been assimilated, do well financially. In other words, it appears possible for them to move into the higher-status majority culture, albeit at the cost of their cultural heritage. The same does not appear to be true of African Americans.

The Educational Hierarchy

Lenski (1966) writes that achievement hierarchies have gained legitimacy over ascriptive hierarchies. These data do not span a long enough period to test this statement, but there is clear indication of the power of achievement systems in the importance of education as a variable. However, as pointed out by Wilson (1978), those on the bottom of the racial/ethnic hierarchy are blocked directly and indirectly from achieving the most desirable ranks in the educational hierarchy. The data here show this to be true. Although each new wave of young

African Americans is more likely to finish high school, the great growth in the education of whites has been in finishing college.

In 1990, 28 percent of white men and 25 percent of white women between the ages of 25 and 49 had completed four years of college or more. By contrast, only 14 percent of African American women, 13 percent of African American men, and 10 percent of Hispanics (men and women) in same age range had done so. However, an undergraduate degree is becoming the minimum entry requirement for middle-class career paths. This does not even begin to take into consideration the difference in *quality* of education available to African Americans. While African American honor graduates from Harvard achieve publicity, most African American students attend inferior high schools, and, partially in consequence of these high schools, less-prominent colleges. Only a few predominately African American universities carry the kind of name recognition that is close to a guarantee of a good career.

Occupation

Occupation is another of the achievement reflecting hierarchies identified by Lenski. However, like education, it is an area in which minorities may be directly and indirectly kept from matching the achievements of whites. Education, (discussed above) is one of the indirect methods. For the oldest African Americans in the country today, a combination of poor education, real or perceived cultural differences (e.g., use of nonstandard English, different views on the centrality of one's job to one's life), and overt discrimination kept them almost castelike in a small number of poorly paid jobs—primarily in service (including household) and unskilled labor. As reported in Chapter 3, at ages 55 to 64, more than half of the African American men in Cohort A were semiskilled or unskilled blue-collar workers, and almost another quarter were in service jobs. At that time 58 percent of African American women in the cohort were in household service. Younger cohorts have moved out of that extremely segregated labor market, but African Americans are still found in very small number in the best-paying and higher-status professional, technical, administrative, and managerial jobs.

The occupational categories chosen for this research were not very sensitive and were only available for the currently employed. The fact of continuing to earn a salary was very important to those beyond age 65. Important for a larger number of people was the existence of a

Despite these limitations, the power of occupation was clearly demonstrated in the fact of income leveling. Racial income differences decline after retirement age because the income of whites drops much more sharply than that of African Americans and Hispanics. This is because, despite larger Social Security payments and greater size and likelihood of pensions and investment income, these sources of income can not begin to compensate for the average white worker's salary.

Gender

Despite the gain in the power of some achievement-based hierarchies, the ascribed status of gender is still a very powerful determinant of income. When personal income is used as a measure, women earn markedly less than men and are segregated into a smaller range of occupations. This is apparent even in the very coarse occupational categories used in this research. Further, the very similar incomes of white, African American, and Hispanic women, compared to the much larger differences in the median incomes of white, African American, and Hispanic men, suggest that gender is more important than race/ethnicity as an ascribed determinant of income. Unlike race, gender does not appear to operate through the educational system, for this great difference in personal income persists in the face of equal or superior education of white and African American women (depending on the measure of educational attainment being used) and the rapid gains of Hispanic women, who have traditionally been less educated than Hispanic men.

Family income, by definition, does not vary between married men and married women. However, in the postretirement ages, unmarried women actually seem to fare better than unmarried men. This is because of the "protective" laws and customs aimed at women in their inferior position. Most unmarried women in these ages are widowed and may have widow's pensions, insurance, and other benefits of their husbands' estates. Though most unmarried men of these ages are also widowed, their wives are unlikely to have held jobs that provided pensions to survivors or substantial insurance, annuities, or other resources. It should be noted that men in the older ages are much less likely to be unmarried than women, so only very small numbers of men are in this disadvantaged status.

Marital Status and Family Support

A related dimension of status, which can be viewed as a mix of ascribed and achieved, is marriage. At both pre- and postretirement ages, it is one of the largest determinants of income. Though not demonstrated in these data, it is also a source of prestige for women in the older age groups. Further, it increases the possibility of maintaining independent living arrangements, which is, in itself, a large source of prestige for the elderly.

Even though living with family members increases the family income pool, independent living is the majority (and preferred) living arrangement for most older adults. For those who cannot live independently (women more often than men, and minority group members more often than whites), living with relatives is preferred to institutionalization or living with nonrelatives (except when the nonrelative is a spouse-like partner).

There are cultural differences in the living arrangements of those who do not live independently. Hispanics (especially Hispanic women) are the most likely to live with relatives, and African Americans (especially African American men) are the most likely to live with nonrelatives. This may be related to the large incidence of divorce and separation among older African Americans, which in turn may lead to poor or nonexistent relations between African American men and the children of these disrupted marriages.

Middle-aged whites, Hispanics, and African Americans are equally likely to have older adults in their homes, despite the higher probability that older Hispanics and African Americans will live with their relatives. This may be largely because of ethnic fertility differences in these older cohorts which spread the "risk" of housing a parent among a larger number of children.. Among Hispanics, it are also many younger families that are not "at risk" because the older generation remains in their country of origin. Despite media stereotypes, those who do provide homes for the elderly are usually those of higher income and smaller family size relative to housing space.

Property

Although the postretirement provisions of the occupation/income system—pensions and Social Security—determine the financial well-being of the greatest number of older adults, property is a hedge against crisis. The single most widely held property of value among elders is their house. More than just the security of a place to live, home ownership provides equity that may be sold or borrowed against to meet financial crisis.

There are large racial/ethnic differences in home ownership, but the degree to which these may be explained by income differences is not examined here. For those who were 65 to 74 in 1980 (Cohort B), over 70 percent of whites were living as head (or spouse) in a home they owned. Only 55 percent of African Americans and just over 45 percent of Hispanics had that arrangement. At older ages, there is some leveling in this variable.

Political/Legal

Across all, or nearly all, of the political spectrum, wealth confers power. Therefore, it is not surprising that even without data on tax deductions and exemptions, which are the largest source of government expenditure on the financially secure elderly, whites receive more money from government programs.

There *is* some protection provided by government programs to the poorest older adults. More minority elders receive need-based programs such as Supplemental Security Income, food stamps, and rent subsidy than white elders, and the median amounts paid to African American and Hispanic elders are higher. However, much more money is paid to older adults through Social Security and government pensions. These go to a larger proportion of whites and in larger median amounts.

Predictions about Future Generations of Elders

The Disclaimer

A number of macroeconomic, political, and social changes may occur before the year 2030, when the youngest person in Cohort M turns 65. The research presented here can shed no light on these and only a dim beam on the future of the micro-level trends it reports. Therefore, like most of my predecessors in the social sciences, I will launch myself off this tiny empirical platform to make some intuitive guesses about the world to come.

Speculations about Future Generations of Older Adults

Older adults in the next 25 to 35 years will be better off than today's elders. For all the stir about how baby boomers will bankrupt Social Security, they will also have too much political clout to allow this branch to be cut out from under them. They may have to accept higher retirement ages and strict prohibitions on government double-dipping as the price of retaining adequate benefits.

I say *may have to accept* higher retirement ages in full realization that sociologists keep writing about how awful mandatory retirement is. Labor force participation rates suggest that better-off men are retiring earlier and earlier. Many people outside the academic world are looking forward to the time when they do not have to get up and go to work. It is the common wisdom among social gerontologists that continuing to work is measurably better for physical health, mental health, and social adjustment, but there are strong parallels between this knowledge and the knowledge that a salad with bean curd followed by a brisk three-mile walk is superior to curling up in bed with a box of chocolates and a trashy novel. The fear of Social Security's bankruptcy will motivate the wealthier members of these cohorts to make larger investments as provisions for their futures, so that the variance in post-retirement income will be larger.

Declines in constant-dollar income for post–baby boom cohorts suggests a bleaker picture for older adults in the more distant future, when their political power may be smaller and their ability to accumulate resources smaller.

Future generations of African Americans will, on average, have higher incomes, and I do not expect to see double jeopardy in the future, just as I do not find it today. However, I expect the amount of leveling to be reduced. Today's young African Americans have escaped the caste boundaries of service worker and manual laborer, which fairly accurately, if stereotypically, characterize today's older African Americans. However, only a very small proportion of the younger African Americans is educationally prepared to assume careers that will allow them much hope of investing for their retirement, even if they face no discrimination in hiring or promotion—an eventuality that will probably not come in their lifetime.

Increasing numbers of Hispanic immigrants from the poorer Latin American countries may lead to conditions becoming worse be-fore they become better for this group. Today's Hispanic elders are probably disproportionately of the more assimilated families. Historically, Mexican immigrants have tended to engage in circular migration during their peak labor force years. They have not remained in the United States to grow old.

The decade from 1980 to 1990 has seen larger numbers of Hispanics living year-round outside of the traditional Hispanic communities. They are raising families in these communities and seem more likely than previous generations of workers to age in place. This may mean more poorly educated and economically disadvantaged Hispanic elders in the future.

At the same time, Hispanics are likely to gain equality of opportunity much faster than African Americans. Their legal protections may be the same, but they will be socially acceptable sooner. Their history will parallel that of the Irish, Italian, and Eastern European Jewish immigrants. As their numbers swell, they excite more prejudice. As they assimilate and, to a lesser extent, small elements of their culture become mainstream "American" (the taco is already as American as pizza), the discrimination will diminish, because, shorn of cultural sign vehicles, they do not look very different from other Americans of European stock, despite the Native American heritage of many whose origins are in Mexico or Central America.

Conclusions

1. Ethnic differences in family income (median and quartile) showed a general, though not always unilateral, decline as the study cohorts aged, supporting the leveling hypothesis.
2. The effect of African American ethnicity on family income, with other sociodemographic variables controlled, was significant at all study ages. Most significant changes were in the direction of reduced influence with age, also supporting the leveling hypothesis.
3. The effect of Hispanic ethnicity is not significant with other sociodemographic variables controlled; however, ethnicity and race are related to substantial differences in educational and occupational opportunities, which translate into strong indirect effects of ethnicity.
4. Income is higher in the younger cohorts, and the direct effect of race on income is smaller. However, equality is not markedly different among the three cohorts.

5. In Cohort B, African Americans and Hispanics have greater numbers in poverty relative to whites after age 65 than in the younger ages, producing a jeopardy of poverty. In Cohort C, the ethnic differences in poverty rates are reduced after age 65, supporting leveling.

6. The direct effects of race/ethnicity (African American and Hispanic) on poverty are significant when other sociodemographic variables are controlled. The effects of ethnicity on poverty are more or less constant over time for Cohort B, supporting neither jeopardy of poverty nor leveling. However, in Cohort C, the effect of ethnicity declines, suggesting leveling.

7. OASDI is the most widespread resource of the elderly. Although whites benefit more than Hispanics and African Americans in both breadth of coverage and amount of benefits, this resource is the major instrument of income leveling.

8. Home ownership is the most important financial asset for older adults. Whites are more likely to own homes at all ages, but there is some leveling after age 75.

9. Though whites are more likely to have other financial assets (savings, stock, bonds) and to have them in larger amounts, the difference in income from these is small. However, the assets themselves, for which income is a proxy measure, represent a cushion for emergencies that protect white elders disproportionately.

10. Most older people live in their own homes, alone or with a spouse. Whites are most likely to have this living arrangement, while Hispanics are more likely than the other groups to live with other family members. With other sociodemographic variables controlled, ethnic differences in living arrangements vary with age, ethnicity, and cohort in no clear pattern.

11. Informed guesses about the future include a higher standard of living for the elderly in general, but very slow reduction (and possibly temporary increase) in inequality, including a reduction in the degree of leveling after age 65.

References

AARP. 1985. Association striving to explode myth. *AARP News Bulletin* 26(2):51.

Anderson, T. A. 1985. The best years of their lives. *Newsweek.* January 7.

Bane, S. D. 1991. Rural minority populations. *Generations* 15(4):63–65.

Belgrave, L. L., M. L. Wykle, and J. M. Choi. 1993. Health, double jeopardy and culture: The use of institutionalization by African-Americans. *The Gerontologist* 33(3):379–85.

Bengtson, V. L. 1979. Ethnicity and aging: Problems and issues in current social science inquiry. Chapter 1 in *Ethnicity and aging: Theory, research, and policy,* ed. D. E. Gelfand and A. J. Kutzik. New York: Springer.

Biafora, F. A., and C. F. Longino, Jr. 1990. Elderly Hispanic migration in the United States. *Journal of Gerontology* 45:S212–19.

Brody, S. J. 1973. Comprehensive health care for the elderly: An analysis. *The Gerontologist* 13(4):142.

Burton, L. M. 1992. Black grandparents rearing children of drug-addicted parents: Stressors, outcomes, and social service needs. *The Gerontologist* 32(6):744–51.

Cherlin, A. J. 1981. *Marriage, divorce, remarriage*. Cambridge, Mass.: Harvard University Press.

Coon, R. 1986. A theoretical examination of double jeopardy: Using theory as guide to concept analysis. *Mid-American Review of Sociology* 11(1):67–90.

Cutler, N. E. 1991. Targeting and means testing, aging and need. *Generations* 15(4):17–18.

Dowd, J. J. 1980. *Stratification among the aged*. Monterey, Calif.: Brooks/Cole.

Dowd J. J., and V. L. Bengtson. 1978. Aging in minority populations: An examination of the double jeopardy hypothesis. *Journal of Gerontology* 33:427–36.

Dressel, P. L. 1986. An overview of the issues. *The Gerontologist* 26(2):128–31.

———. 1988. Gender, race, and class: Beyond the feminization of poverty in later life. *The Gerontologist* 28(2):177–80.

Duffy M., E. Barrington, J. M. Flanagan, and L. Olson. 1980. *Inflation and the elderly*. Part 1: *Summary report*. Part 2: *Main report*. Part 3: *Appendices*. Prepared for NRTA-AARP, Washington, D.C. Lexington, Mass.: Data Resources.

Elder, G. H. 1974. *Children of the great depression: Social change in life experience*. Chicago: University of Chicago Press.

Featherman, D. L., and R. M. Hauser. 1976. Changes in the socio-economic stratification of the races, 1962–73. *American Journal of Sociology* 82:621–49.

Ferraro, K. F. 1987. Double jeopardy to health for Black older adults? *Journal of Gerontology* 42:528–33.

Ford, A. B., M. R. Haug, P. K. Jones, A. W. Roy, and S. J. Folmar. 1990. Race-related differences among elderly urban residents: A cohort study, 1975–1984. *Journal of Gerontology* 45:S163–71.

Fox, P. D., and S. B. Clauser. 1980. Trends in nursing home expenditures: Implications for aging policy. *Health Care Financing Review*, Fall, 65–70.

Gelfand, D. E., and C. M. Barresi. 1987. Introduction. In *Ethnic dimensions of aging*, ed. D. E. Gelfand and C. M. Barresi. New York: Springer.

Gibson, R. C. 1991a. Race and the self-reported health of elderly persons. *Journal of Gerontology* 46:S235–42.

———. 1991b. The subjective retirement of Black Americans. *Journal of Gerontology* 46:S204–9.

Gibson, R. C., and C. J. Burns. 1991. The health, labor force, and retirement experiences of aging minorities. *Generations* 15(4):31–35.

Gould, W. B., IV. 1993. *A primer on American labor law*. 3d ed. Cambridge, Mass.: MIT Press.

Green, J. W. 1989. Aging and ethnicity: An emergent issue in social gerontology. *Journal of Cross-Cultural Gerontology* 4:377–83.

Grizzell, E. D. 1923. *Origin and development of the high school in New England before 1865*. New York: Macmillan.

Hanushek, E. A., and J. E. Jackson. 1977. *Statistical methods for social sciences*. New York: Academic Press.

Health Care Financing Administration. 1985. Health care financing trends. *Health Care Financing Review* 6(3):89–98.

Hernandez, J., L. Estrada, and D. Alvirez. 1973. Census data and the problem of conceptually defining the Mexican American population. *Social Science Quarterly* 53(4):671–87.

Hofferth, S. L. 1984. Kin networks, race and family structure. *Journal of Marriage and the Family* 46(4):791–816.

Hoover, S. L. 1981. Black and Spanish elderly: Their housing characteristics and housing quality. In *Community housing choices for older Americans*, ed. M. P. Lawton and S. L. Hoover. New York: Springer.

Hurd, M. D. 1989. The economic status of the elderly. *Science* 244:659–64.

Jackson, J. J. 1971. Negro aged: Toward needed research in social gerontology. *The Gerontologist* 11(Spring):52–57.

———. 1972. Black aged: In quest of the phoenix. In *Triple jeopardy—Myth or reality*, ed. National Council on the Aging. Washington, D.C.: National Council on the Aging.

———. 1980. *Minorities and aging.* Belmont, Calif.: Wadsworth.

Jackson, M., and J. L. Wood. 1976. *Aging in America: Implications for the Black aged.* Washington, D.C.: National Council on the Aging.

Jackson, M., B. Kolody, and J. L. Wood. 1982. To be old and black: The case for double jeopardy on income and health. In *Minority aging: Sociological and social psychological issues*, ed. R. C. Manuel. Westport, Conn.: Greenwood Press.

Johanningmeir, E. V. 1980. *Americans and their schools.* Chicago: Rand McNally.

Johnson, J. A., H. W. Collins, V. L. Dupuis, and J. H. Johansen. 1969. *Introduction to the foundation of American education.* Boston: Allyn and Bacon.

Johnson, R. J., and F. D. Wolinsky. 1994. Gender, race, and health: The structure of health status among older adults. *The Gerontologist* 34(1):24–35.

Kamikawa, L. 1991. Public entitlements: Exclusionary beneficence. *Generations* 15(4):21–24.

Kanellos, N., ed. 1993. *The Hispanic-American almanac: A reference work on Hispanics in the U.S.* Detroit, Mich.: Gale Research.

Kent, D. P. 1971a. The elderly in minority groups: Variant patterns of aging. *The Gerontologist* 11 (Spring):26–29.

———. 1971b. The Negro aged. *The Gerontologist* 11(Spring):48–51.
Kett, J. F. 1977. *Rites of passage: Adolescence in America 1790 to the present*. New York: Basic Books.
King, D. K. 1988. Multiple jeopardy, multiple consciousness: The context of a black feminist ideology. *Signs: Journal of Women in Culture and Society* 14(1):42–72.
Knight, E. W. 1922. *Public education in the South*. Boston: Ginn.
Krause, N. 1993. Race differences in life satisfaction among aged men and women. *Journal of Gerontology* 48:S235–44.
Kreps, J. M. 1976. *Women and the American economy: A look to the 1980's*. Englewood Cliffs, N.J.: Prentice-Hall.
LaVor, J. 1979. Long term care: A challenge to the service system. In *Reform and regulation in long term care,* ed. V. LaPorte and J. Rubin. New York: Praeger.
Lenski, G. 1966. *Power and privilege*. New York: McGraw Hill.
Levin, J. S., and R. J. Taylor. 1993. Gender and age differences in religiosity among Black Americans. *The Gerontologist* 33(1):16–23.
Longino, C. F., Jr., and K. J. Smith. 1991. Black retirement migration in the United States. *Journal of Gerontology* 46:S125–32.
Madison, A. 1992. The social contract and the African American elderly. *Urban League Review* 15(2):21–28.
Manuel, R. C. 1982. *Minority aging: Sociological and social psychological issues*. Westport, Conn.: Greenwood Press.
Markides, K. S., H. W. Martin, and E. Gomez. 1983. *Older Mexican Americans: A study in an urban barrio*. Austin, Texas: Center for Mexican American Studies, University of Texas at Austin.
Minkler, M. 1991. Generational equity or interdependence? *Generations* 15(4):36, 40–42.
Minkler, M., K. M. Roe, and M. Price. 1992. The physical and emotional health of grandmothers raising grandchildren in the crack cocaine epidemic. *The Gerontologist* 32(6):752–61.
Mitchell, J., and J. C. Register. 1984. An exploration of family interaction with the elderly by race, socioeconomic status, and residence. *The Gerontologist* 24(1):48–54.
Moon, M. 1977. *The measure of economic welfare: Its application to the aged poor*. New York: Academic Press.
Moore, J. W. 1971. Mexican Americans. *The Gerontologist* 11(Spring):30–35.

National Committee against Discrimination in Housing. 1968. *The impact of housing patterns on job opportunities.* New York: National Committee against Discrimination in Housing.

National Council on the Aging. 1972. *Triple jeopardy—Myth or reality.* Washington, D.C.: National Council on the Aging.

Nava, J. 1975. Educational challenges in elementary and secondary schools. In *Mexican Americans tomorrow*, ed. G. Tyler. Albuquerque: University of New Mexico Press.

Nelson, G. M. 1983. Tax expenditures for the elderly. *The Gerontologist* 23(5): 471–78.

Nevin, D., and R. E. Bills. 1976. *The schools that fear built: Segregationist academies in the South.* Washington, D.C.: Acropolis Books.

Northrup, H. R. 1944. *Organized labor and the Negro.* New York: Harper and Brothers.

O'Rand, A. M. 1982. Socioeconomic status and poverty. In *Social roles and social participation,* ed. D. J. Mangen and W. A. Peterson. Minneapolis: University of Minnesota Press.

Padgett, D. 1988. Aging minority women: Issues in research and health policy. *Women and Health* 14(3–4):213–24.

Palmore, E., and K. Manton. 1973. Ageism compared to racism and sexism. *Journal of Gerontology* 28:363–69.

Pampel, F. C. 1981. *Social change and the aged.* Lexington, Mass.: Lexington Books.

Pies, H. E. 1984. Life care communities for the aged: An overview. In *Long term care financing and delivery systems: Exploring some alternatives*, ed. P. H. Feinstein, M. Gornick, and J. N. Greenberg. Proceedings from a conference held January 24, Baltimore, Md.: Dept. of Health and Human Services, Health Care Financing Administration; Washington, D.C.: U. S. Government Printing Office.

Projector, D. S., and G. S. Weiss. 1966. *Survey of financial characteristics of consumers.* Washington, D.C.: Board of Governors of the Federal Reserve System.

Riley, M. W. 1971a. *Aging and society III.* New York: Russell Sage Foundation.

———. 1971b. Social gerontology and the age stratification of society. *The Gerontologist* 11(Spring):79–87.

———. 1976. Age strata in social systems. In *Handbook on aging and the social sciences,* ed. R. H. Binstock and E. Shanas. New York: Van Nostrand Reinhold.

Rodeheaver, D., and N. Datan. 1988. The challenge of double jeopardy: Toward a mental health agenda for aging women. *American Psychologist* 43(8):648–54.

Saenz, D. 1972. Triple jeopardy—Myth or reality? In *Triple jeopardy—Myth or reality,* ed. National Council on the Aging. Washington, D.C.: National Council on the Aging.

Samora, J. 1975. Mexican immigration. In *Mexican Americans tomorrow*, ed. G. Tyler. Albuquerque: University of New Mexico Press.

Sherman, S. R. 1985. Assets of new retired-worker beneficiaries: Findings from the new beneficiary survey. *Social Security Bulletin* 48(7):27–43.

Snyder, D. C. 1979. Future pension status of the black elderly. In *Ethnicity and aging: Theory, research, and policy*, ed. D. E. Gelfand and A. J. Kalzik. New York: Springer

Social Security Administration. 1985. Current operating statistics. *Social Security Bulletin* 48(1):31–67.

Spero, S. D., and A. L. Harris. 1931. *The Black worker: A study of the negro and the labor movement*. New York: Columbia University Press.

Stanford, E. P., and D. L. Yee. 1991. Gerontology and the relevance of diversity. *Generations* 15(4):11–14.

Staples, R., and A. Mirande. 1980. Racial and cultural variations among American families. *Journal of Marriage and the Family* 42(11):887–903.

Taeuber, C. 1990. Diversity: The dramatic reality. In *Diversity in Aging,* ed. S. A. Bass, E. A. Kutza, and F. M. Torres-Gil. Glenview, Ill.: Scott, Foresman.

Tienda, M., and R. Angel. 1982. Headship and household composition among Blacks, Hispanics, and other whites. *Social Forces* 61(Dec.):508–31.

Torres-Gil, F. 1986. An examination of factors affecting future cohorts of elderly Hispanics. *The Gerontologist* 26(2):140–46.

Troll, L. E. 1971. The family of later life: A decade review. *Journal of Marriage and the Family* 33(5):263–290.

U.S. Bureau of the Census. 1972a. *Census of population and housing, 1960 public use sample*. [Machine-readable data file.] Prepared by

National Data Use and Access Laboratories. Arlington, Va.: Dualabs.

———. 1972b. *Public use samples of basic records from the 1970 census, description and technical documentation.* Washington, D.C.: U.S. Department of Commerce.

———. 1973a. *Census of population: 1970.* Vol. 1. *Characteristics of the population.* Part 6 (California), Part 11 (Florida), Part 45 (Texas), and Part 36 (New York). Washington, D.C.: U.S. Department of Commerce.

———. 1973b. *Census of population: 1970.* Vol. 1, *Characteristics of the Population.* Part 1, United States Summary—Section 2. Washington, D.C.: U.S. Department of Commerce.

———. 1973c. *Technical documentation for the 1960 public use sample. PUS–1960.* Prepared by National Data Use and Access Laboratories. Rosslyn, Va.: Dualabs.

———. 1981a. *Current population survey, March 1980.* [Machine-readable data file.] Conducted by the Bureau of the Census for the Bureau of Labor Statistics, Revised Edition. Washington, D. C: U.S. Bureau of the Census.

———.1981b. *Current population survey, March 1980: Tape technical documentation.* Prepared by Data Access and Use Staff, Data User Services Division, Bureau of the Census. Washington, D.C.: U.S. Bureau of the Census.

———. 1983a. *Census of population and housing, 1980: Public use microdata sample* (A). [Machine-readable data file.] Prepared by the Bureau of the Census. Washington, D.C.: U.S. Bureau of the Census.

———. 1983b. *Census of population and housing, 1980: Public use microdata sample technical documentation.* Prepared by the Data Users Service Division, Bureau of the Census. Washington, D.C.: U.S. Bureau of the Census.

———. 1984. *1980 Census of population.* Vol. 1, *Characteristics of the population.* Chapter D: Detailed population characteristics. Part 1, United States Summary. PC80-1-D1-A. Washington, D.C.: U.S. Bureau of the Census.

———. 1991. *Current population reports,* Series R-60, Table No. 174. Washington, D.C.: U.S. Government Printing Office.

———. 1992a. *1990 Census of population.* General population characteristics: United States. 1990 CP-1-1. Washington, D.C.: U.S. Bureau of the Census.

———. 1992b. *Census of populaton and housing, 1990: Public use microdata samples, U.S.* [Machine-readable data files.] Prepared by the Bureau of the Census. Washington, D.C.: U.S. Bureau of the Census.

———. 1992c. *Census of populaton and housing, 1990: Public use microdata samples, U.S. technical documentation*. Prepared by the Bureau of the Census. Washington, D.C.: U.S. Bureau of the Census.

———. 1992d. *Current population reports*, Series P-20, Table No. 462. Washington, D.C.: U.S. Government Printing Office.

U.S. Senate, Special Committee on Aging; American Association of Retired Persons; Federal Council on the Aging; and U.S. Administration on Aging. 1991. *Aging America: Trends and projections (1991 edition)*. Washington, D.C.: U.S. Department of Health and Human Services.

Watson, W. H. 1986. Crystal ball gazing: Notes on today's middle aged Blacks with implications for their aging in the 21st century. *The Gerontologist* 26(2):136–39.

Weissert, W. G. 1981. Toward a continuum of care for the elderly: A note of caution. *Public Policy* 29(3):331–40.

———. 1983. Innovative approaches to long-term care and their evaluation. Paper presented to the Conference on the Impact of Technology on Aging in America, February 16–18, Millwood, Va.

———. 1984. Long-term care: Current policy and further directions. Presented to the Seminar Series, Northwestern University. Evanston, Ill.

Weissert, W., and W. Scanlon. 1982. Determinants of institutionalization of the aged. Urban Institute Working Paper, no. 1466-21. Washington, D.C.: Urban Institute.

Wilson, W. J. 1978. *The declining significance of race*. Chicago: University of Chicago Press.

———. 1980. *The declining significance of race*. Rev. ed. Chicago: University of Chicago Press.

Index

Note: All topics refer to comparisons among African Americans, Hispanics, and whites.